THE FUTURE OF AGRICULTURE
IN THE ROCKY MOUNTAINS

This publication resulted from papers presented at
The Future of Agriculture in the Rocky Mountains (FARM)
October 24-22, 1979, Sun Valley, Idaho
a conference sponsored by
The Institute of the American West
a division of the Sun Valley Center for the Arts and Humanities
and was made possible by grants from
The Association for the Humanities in Idaho
a state-based program of
The National Endowment for the Humanities
and by
Levi Strauss & Co.

the Future of Agriculture in the Rocky Mountains

Edited and With an Introduction by

E. Richard Hart

WESTWATER PRESS, INC.
Salt Lake City & Chicago

1980

Library of Congress Catalog Card No. 80-23242

Published by Westwater Press, Inc.
Post Office Box 6394
Salt Lake City, Utah 84106

Manufactured in the United States of America

LIBRARY OF CONGRESS CATALOGING IN PUBLICATION DATA

The Future of Agriculture in the Rocky Mountains

    1. Agriculture and state—Rocky Mountain region—Addresses,
essays, lectures.   2. Agriculture—Rocky Mountain region—Addresses,
essays, lectures.   3. Rocky Mountain region—Public lands—Addresses,
essays, lectures.   I. Hart, E. Richard.

HD1773.A7F87   338.1'0978   80-23242

ISBN 0-935704-05-1

Contents

Range Country Wisdom

You take a good dog...
You don't give him nothin' to do...
He'll go to killin' sheep.

Drum Hadley

E. Richard Hart is the former Director of the Institute of the American West in the Sun Valley Institute of the Arts and Humanities. He has published poetry, history, and essays and has contributed to a number of Native American tribal histories. He is currently at work on a history of the Zuni Indians of New Mexico.

Alvin M. Josephy, Jr. is the former Editor of *American Heritage* magazine. His many works include *Red Power: The American Indians' Fight for Freedom; The Patriot Chiefs; The Indian Heritage of America;* and *History of the Congress of the United States.* He was an Associate Editor of *Time* from 1951 to 1960. He is currently Director of the Institute of the American West.

Drum Hadley is an Arizona poet and rancher.

Introduction

E. Richard Hart

The history of the Rocky Mountain region is one of farming and ranching. The culture of this region is *agriculture*. The fabric and knit of this region are woven from planting to harvest. There are plenty of physical resources in this arid, relatively sparsely populated part of the world, but there is only one essential resource— agriculture.

Many centuries before the first Europeans invaded the Intermountain West, the science of agriculture had already begun. A number of Rocky Mountain tribes were engaged in agricultural pursuits before the first white men arrived. In what is now Utah, Southern Paiutes and Utes planted corn and dug irrigation ditches in the spring, next to the brown runoff of creeks and rivers. In New Mexico, Zuni farmers built low mud walls to prevent the wind from blowing away precious topsoil; they packed arroyos with brush, making dams to prevent the topsoil from washing away; and they utilized every available drop of water in their territory in order to grow their crops (often hand-watering each individual plant), practicing efficient erosion control at the same time. Many tribes throughout the Intermountain West had domesticated animals that they ranged across the inland plains.

The first Europeans to enter the region were Spanish, who arrived in the mid-sixteenth century, bringing, along with disease and servitude, new crops and new animals—especially horses and sheep. From that time until the fur trappers' arrival in the nineteenth century, many tribes subsisted by ranging stock, growing

[1]

crops, and hunting with horses bred from animals that escaped from the Spanish during the Pueblo Revolt of 1680. When the first groups of trappers came into the area in groups of hundreds with huge herds of livestock (unlike Hollywood's Jeremiah Johnson), much of the land was already in agricultural use.

Major ecological damage to the environment of the Rocky Mountain agricultural land began with the arrival of the trappers. British companies were ordered to carry out a "scorched stream" policy to make the area less attractive to American trappers. They methodically killed game and destroyed growth. Before the end of the 1830s much of the normal harvest of grass seed by Northern Paiutes and Western Shoshone in Nevada had been disrupted or destroyed. The Humboldt drainage would never again have chest-high grass or support grazing buffalo and other big game. Beaver were virtually wiped out in Idaho. The trappers under Peter Skene Ogden brought hundreds of deer tongues into camp as proof of their slaughter, severely depleting herds in some areas.

During most of the subsequent immigration to the Intermountain states, people were leaving a condition they perceived as chaos and disorder in the East and were attempting to find a more orderly life, a life with better *quality* in the West.

Small communities and towns of Spaniards, Germans, Scandinavians—people of many faiths, from several continents—began to dot the valleys, mountains, and deserts of the Intermountain West. These farmers and settlers made many mistakes, often mistreating and sometimes eliminating the native inhabitants. Sometimes there was great friction between the immigrants' own different ethnic or national groups. Nevertheless, it was these farmers and ranchers who "won" this West. It was not federal troops who "tamed" most of the landscape in Montana, Utah, Nevada, and Arizona; it was common workers—ranchers, farmers, miners, and entrepreneurs— often disgusted with anarchic conditions in the East and after freedom on the "frontier."

But most of these immigrants were used to a humid region, where irrigation was unnecessary and rainfall was heavy. The high grass in the fields of Utah fooled the Mormons, who overgrazed it within two generations. Waving fields of grass were replaced with broad stretches of sagebrush. Juniper began to creep down the sides of the hills. The cattlemen and sheepmen who drove their huge herds into Montana, Wyoming, and Idaho also misjudged the carrying capacity of the land.

There were some who recognized the situation for what it was. John Wesley Powell's report on the arid lands of the West was presented to Congress in 1879. He suggested new methods for dealing with the environment in the Mountain states. But Powell's suggestions were mostly ignored. The government continued to encourage improper use of western rangelands and farmlands. Navajos were encouraged to keep vast flocks of sheep—until the land was nearly destroyed. Then the Indians had to watch the government destroy the very flocks they had been encouraged to breed. Still they survived on ranching and farming, as the other Rocky Mountain tribes were doing. Southern Paiutes, Western Shoshone, Northern Paiutes, and Utes began to farm with more efficient white agricultural methods. Consequently, over the past hundred years the economy at reservations such as Duck Valley (on the Idaho/Nevada border) has become wholly dependent on agriculture.

Many agricultural lands of the West continued to deteriorate through the early twentieth century. But cattlemen and farmers who were to survive had to learn to be "conservationists" and "environmentalists." Rangelands that had been "up for grabs" now began to come under control from the federal government, and in 1934 the Taylor Grazing Act placed more controls on the air public lands of the mountain states.

Most experts agree that the rangelands in the West are in better shape today than in any period since the 1930s. Some claim that these lands, properly managed, could support nearly twice as much livestock as they do today.

Row-crop farming has grown along with ranching in the Rocky Mountains. Reclamation projects throughout the first half of this century opened up irrigated farmland to thousands of immigrant families (both from this country and abroad). The development of high-lift pumps in the 1960s increased again the amount of land under cultivation.

The history of this region *is* the history of farming and ranching. But things are now changing. Pressures from a multitude of directions threaten the survival of the ranching/farming culture and economy in the Intermountain states.

For the purposes of this publication, the threats and contemporary conflicts have been grouped into four broad categories: (1) *Physical Resources,* (2) *Human Resources,* (3) *Food and Politics* and (4) *The Sagebrush Rebellion.*

Physical Resources

Poet Wendell Berry made the following comment in *The Unsettling of America:*

> My point is that food is a cultural product: It cannot be produced by technology alone. Those agriculturalists who think of the problems of food production solely in terms of technological innovation are oversimplifying.... There are agricultural disciplines that have nothing to do with crop production, just as there are agricultural obligations that belong to people who are not farmers.[1]

Although the physical resources of the Rocky Mountains have been among the last in the United States to be fully exploited, throughout the past century farming and ranching in the area have developed to a point where most of the resources are utilized and a whole economic system has been created. The agriculture in the region developed in part because the "highest and best" use for land and water has traditionally been considered to be for ranching and farming, for raising the food and wool that fed and clothed us. Now there is increasing competition for both land and water. And agricultural problems that are critical in the Midwest or East are exacerbated by the aridity of the Rocky Mountain region.

In the Mountain states, where rainfall is slight—four to twelve inches a year in much of the region—irrigation is absolutely necessary to most profitable agriculture. But water is scarce and valuable. In fact, to farmers in the dry Mountain states, water is everything. Yet there are threats to the entire existing supply of water in the region. For example, the Snake River Aquifer, which feeds one of the largest rivers systems in the West, flows 500 to 600 feet below the surface of the Idaho National Engineering Laboratory (INEL) testing grounds, where INEL has been testing nuclear reactors since 1949. In a poll conducted in conjunction with the FARM project that produced the body of work in this book, we asked Idaho residents if they thought waste-disposal practices of INEL posed a threat to the Snake River Aquifer. Seventy-four percent of the respondents reported they did believe there were threats. At the FARM conference, held in October 1979, at which the papers included in this book were delivered, I asked two of the participants what they thought. Both Dr. Rupert Cutler, Assistant Secretary of Agriculture for Natural Resources and

Environment, and Mr. R. Keith Higginson, United States Commissioner of Reclamation, had answers. Cutler responded, "I don't think that's a question that lends itself to a public-opinion poll. I think that's a technical question." Higginson, it turned out, had been a member of a panel that examined that very question some years ago. He said, "There was concern over the practices of INEL on the burial ground, whether that burial ground was a safe place to store low-level radioactive wastes and those high-level radioactive wastes that were put in storage containers. We looked into it and it was our conclusion at that time that the practice was satisfactory." He did suggest that more monitoring was necessary.

In November 1979, only a few days after the FARM conference, investigative reporters dropped a bombshell on the public who lived in the Snake River and Columbia Basin drainages. *Sixteen billion gallons of liquid radioactive waste had been discharged into Idaho's Snake River Aquifer between 1952 and 1970.* Strontium 90 and hexavalent chromium had been piped into the 9,600-mile-square aquifer through disposal wells. One hundred million pounds of chemicals and seventy thousand curies of radiation had been discharged into the ground above the aquifer. Tritium and salt, also used in the production of nuclear power, had contaminated areas at INEL. These materials did not leak into the aquifer; they were intentionally injected, often under pressure.

Thus far refusing to alter its practices drastically, INEL continues to discharge radioactive waste into the aquifer.

One need only look at a map to see the importance of this water system. The water of the aquifer feeds the Snake River from the Grand Tetons, flows beneath INEL to Thousand Springs and Blue Lakes, pours into the Snake, which then cuts its way across Idaho, through Hell's Canyon (where hardy ranchers run their cattle in the summer, and have for a hundred years) and the Columbia River Gorge, past Portland and Old Fort Stevens, and into the Pacific Ocean.

Some investors, noting the skyrocketing value of gold, have found it a hedge against inflation, an investment matching the soaring cost of living. Even so, in the Rocky Mountain states there may come a time when no amount of gold will buy any amount of water. Water comes in a finite supply in this part of the country. As the price of gold rises, it again becomes profitable to reopen mines, closed since the turn of the century. But as the price of water rises, no new or old, unused sources of water will be discovered. Little more can be brought up from the ground through high-lift wells without depleting other known sources. And in some areas, despite all efforts, water tables are dropping dangerously. Yet for agriculture in the West to survive, there cannot be *investment* in water, because if there is, uses like the production of power will strip the dry earth of all available moisture, bringing fantastic profit to special interests but wiping out irrigated agriculture. Individual farmers will not be able to compete with the giant conglomerates producing power. *If decisions are made solely on the basis of economics, irrigated fields may not survive in the Rocky Mountain region.*

Power companies, mining interests, and even other regions' agricultural concerns covet the water that Intermountain farmers have used for generations. Agriculture is no longer considered the highest and best use for Rocky Mountain water—at least not by many in regions outside the Intermountain states. Complex maneuverings between power companies, farmers, and irrigation companies (such as the suit involving Idaho Power and other users of the Snake River) may determine who will control that water in the future. There is also pressure to use Idaho and Wyoming water to supply other regions, for gasification plants, coal slurries, synthetic-fuel plants, and coal-fired power plants. In early December 1979 Secretary of the Interior Andrus approved a 3,000-megawatt complex of coal-fired power plants in the western Utah desert. At full production, this $4.5 billion complex—the world's largest—will generate as much electricity in a day as the entire state of Utah uses in a year. Ultimately, the issue may boil down to the survival either of these plants or of green plants.

And Rocky Mountain water faces still other threats. There are even plans to divert enormous amounts of that water to California for agricultural use. Ten years ago a bipartisan effort of Idaho republicans and democrats led by Len Jordan and Frank Church managed to place a moratorium on plans to build a giant canal, on a scale with the Alaska Pipeline, which could have sent millions of acre feet of Snake River water to Lake Mead and eventually on to California. Recently the moratorium was extended.

One might wonder whether such a project is fantasy or possibility, but now a new disclosure has revealed that the Environmental Protection Agency was conducting a study on diverting additional Idaho water to other regions. One poll found that 80 percent of

the public was against any such diversion. Writer Grace Lichten-
stein echoed an old concern of the West when she commented,
"Water usually flows downhill, except when it flows uphill toward
money."

Prime farmland in the region has become similarly scarce.
Many uses seem to be taking precedence over farming. Nor are oil
shale, coal, gas liquification, and strip mining the only competitors
for prime farmland. Clean air, a relatively low cost of living, and
sparse population have led many to immigrate into the Rocky Mountain states in the past decade. Idaho's population has shot up at 6
percent a year. Blaine County in that state has grown 50 percent
in the last seven years and may grow another 100 percent by the
year 2000. The explosive growth of urban communities in states like
Idaho has begun to gobble up the best farmland at an astounding
rate. In Utah the entire Wasatch Front, once the "breadbasket" of
the Mormon heartland, is now Ogden, Salt Lake City, Sandy, Provo,
and their respective suburbs. The prime Snake River and Columbia
River drainage farmland is similarly threatened.

Assistant Secretary of Agriculture Rupert Cutler has spent
years striving to protect our nation's wilderness areas and has had a
major impact on the history of public lands. From him we learn that
3 million acres a year are lost to homes, businesses, roads, and ponds.
The amount of *prime* cropland is going down as well. It seems that
both quality and quantity are on the decline. Soil erosion is also a
severe threat to Rocky Mountain range and cropland. And, as Cutler
reminds us, "More than half of the nation's cropland, forests, pastures,
and rangeland need increased conservation treatment to reduce soil
erosion and improve water quality." Guy Martin, Assistant Secretary
of the Interior for Land and Water Resources, agreed, calling the
condition of the public rangeland in the Western states "deplorable,"
and adding that 80 percent of the land is in fair, poor, or bad condition. In fact, some experts claim that *desertification* is taking
place in the West. But others argue that we should not preach doom,
reminding us that western lands are in better condition than they
have been in fifty years.

Native American farmers see many of the same problems.
Shoshone leader Washakie once summed up his profound distaste
for agriculture with the statement, "God damn a potato!" Things
are different today and have been for a long time. The Native Americans in the Rocky Mountains are not only the original residents of

the region but are also the first settlers and among the first farmers. The history of the Rocky Mountain tribes over the past seventy-five years has been one of ranching and farming. Today they are feeling many of the same pressures as white farmers—and some additional ones. Tribes are renewing efforts to bring about the enforcement of the Winters Doctrine (a Supreme Court ruling guaranteeing tribes the right to water flowing on or adjacent to their reservations for all time). The tribes are feeling pressures from recreationalists, too. At Duck Valley, for instance, Nevada business and political interests are trying to force irrigation water from the tribe's Wildhorse Reservoir and into recreational use. The tribe also fears that a proposed nuclear-power plant will deplete tribal waters. Even a casino is attempting to gain access to the water in order to build a resort on the lake.

Human Resources

Author Alvin M. Josephy, Jr., gave an overview of the changes taking place in the West when he said;

> Fundamentally, what is happening is that a colonialistic society —still ruggedly individualist, but nevertheless dependent on decision-making elsewhere—is being dispossessed, just as it once dispossessed the Indian, and a culture based on a ranching/ farming economy is being supplanted by one based on industry and technology.[2]

In his 1978 State of the Union address, President Carter declared, "What's best for farm families in the long run is also best for the consumers." More than 60 percent of the respondents to a Harris poll indicated that they also support the preservation of the family farm and would even be willing to pay 5 percent more for their food to demonstrate that support. People in Idaho share those beliefs. In a 1976 poll 96 percent of the Idaho population reported that they wanted to see at least as much farming in the state twenty years from now, and 75 percent said they wanted to see *more* farming by that time. The overwhelming majority of the population of this Rocky Mountain state want to see an economy based on ranching and farming. It makes sense in other ways as well. Experts on world hunger tell us that large agribusiness farms are not as efficient as the family farm.

Even so, a great number of policies and issues seem to threaten the existence of the family farm, especially in the Rocky Mountain region. Some are already calling the family farm a "dinosaur." Much of the cultural heritage and many of the valued traits in western society come from the legacy left us by the family farm. But it is getting more and more difficult for a young person to find the capital necessary to start ranching or farming. The technology used in farming is advancing at blinding speed (although that technology might not always be appropriate today). Land is unavailable and when inherited is often too expensive to keep. To top it off, as Thadis W. Box reported in a recent lecture,

> Realistically, the future of the arid lands of the western United States will be controlled by people who reside in the cities of the West and in the more populated areas of the eastern and western United States. Policies are likely to be made primarily on what these people perceive the problems to be, rather than the reality of the problems themselves.[3]

Catholic Bishop George H. Speltz recently said that the trends toward consolidation and increasing absentee ownership of productive farmland "erode whatever economic power remains in the hands of rural people and, if carried far enough, would permit the rise in nonmetropolitan America of a sort of landed gentry."[4]

It was a great treat for the FARM conferees to meet and hear poet and rancher Drummond Hadley, who has contributed poems for this publication. Drum ranches in southernmost Arizona and writes some of the most beautiful and evocative poetry ever written about the West. He is an empathic man, and his reading immediately won over most of the large audience. After his reading, I told him that I had read in a newspaper that he had once fired off a revolver into the air during a reading at Bisbee, Arizona. "Why didn't *we* get any gunfire?" I asked. "Oh," he said, "I lost that poem." We may not have seen any gunfire, but we were witness to probably the only time a "filly" has been roped with a rawhide lariat in the Sun Valley Opera House. Another contributor to this publication, environmentalist Clancy Gordon, said at the conference that one of humankind's worse problems was that people seem able to adapt to and endure almost unbelievable environments. But the ranchers and farmers I met at this conference, Drummond among them, seemed to be people who would not adapt easily.

Food and Politics

William Jennings Bryan once said,

The great cities rest upon our broad and fertile prairies. Burn down your cities and leave our farms, and your cities will spring up again as if by magic; but destroy our farms, and the grass will grow in the streets of every city in the country.

Bryan said that in 1896. Unfortunately, however, in the last eighty years the public has achieved no greater awareness of this situation. On the contrary, there seems to be less general awareness of agriculture, agricultural practices, and nutrition than in Bryan's day.

How is it that the farmer could come to be in this absurd position: enjoying almost universal popular support, but encountering every imaginable economic obstacle? One answer is, of course, "politics."

Severe droughts in the mid-1960s caused starvation and threatened even worse disaster on the Indian subcontinent. Fortunately, U.S. food reserves and surpluses came to the rescue, saving millions of lives. Prognosticators saw the 1970s filled with world famine and starvation. But the "Green Revolution" (technological advances in agriculture) held back that famine for a few years. Hopes rose. Then, in 1972, worldwide crop failures threatened the lives of millions. Russian representatives secretly arranged a deal with U.S. grain dealers in which far more wheat was sold to the U.S.S.R. than the United States could afford to lose without depleting its reserve. As a result, wheat reserves in the world were depleted to the lowest level in twenty-one years. The U.S. wheat stockpiles were reduced from 26 million metric tons in 1972 to 9 million in 1974. The result was higher prices for wheat—from \$1.57/bushel to \$4.48/bushel. Then Secretary of Agriculture Earl Butz told farmers, "Low prices are a thing of the past." The government predicted that the world market would buy everything that U.S. farmers could grow. They should plant "fencerow to fencerow."

But public agencies responded when bread rose three to ten cents a loaf. Paranoid consumer groups predicted the \$1 loaf of bread, and the Ford Administration, bowing to pressure, implemented a grain embargo. The bottom fell out of the market. Farmers had little to do with any of the politics and, though for a brief time they made a decent profit, the real profiteering went on in the packaging industries and among wheat dealers and political insiders.

Did consumers have a right to feel so strongly about the three-cent increase in the cost of bread? In the United States we spend about 17 percent of our disposable income for food. In Russia, it is 53 percent. In England, 25 percent. In Asia it is roughly 82 percent. In fact, U.S. food has risen at a lower rate than practically any other commodity in the past century.

Some easterners have complained that the problems of the farmer's income are caused largely by his ignorance of the first rule of capitalism: "To ensure a profit, supply must not exceed demand." "He is a compulsive overproducer," say these critics, and for the past fifty years government farm policy has tried to compensate for this by providing incentives to limit production. Opponents of that argument say that the farmer does not control the market, that it is not a "free" market, that politicians listen more attentively to Betty Furness and the consumer than to farmers. To tell the farmer to be less efficient or to cut his production in half may be like telling General Motors to drive half their Chevrolets off a cliff in order to increase the value of the remaining cars. If the family farm is to survive, these voices claim, the politician must refrain from manipulating food prices in order to secure his/her reelection. In 1979 wheat prices were up again.

During 1979 the Carter Administration revealed its plan to build a huge "racetrack" system for missiles in the Utah and Nevada deserts. Called the MX (Missile Experimental) System, the plan calls for placing 200 mobile missiles randomly among 4,600 shelters, on loops off the "racetrack." The whole operation would cover ten thousand miles and would need 172 billion gallons of water for construction and operation. Initially Nevada and Utah officials expressed support for the plans but when the magnitude of the project became known, support began to dwindle. The Air Force claims that the most extensive environmental impact study ever made has been completed in advance of this project, but critics say that no conceivable plan could cause more damage to the fragile valleys of the semiarid desert in the Great Basin.

In December 1979 it was learned that the system would be built within a short distance of major population centers in Utah. But many residents of Utah and Nevada, remembering the military's promises in the past and having seen their families sicken and die from radiation-related diseases caused by above-ground testing of nuclear weapons, are opposed. In March 1980, Congressional auditors said that the system would cost at least $56 billion and not the $33 billion estimated by the administration. Opponents claim that the MX would cost in excess of $100 billion—the biggest public-works project in history. But beyond the question of cost, the General Accounting Office has expressed doubts about whether the missile system would even work. State officials are rapidly turning against the idea. Even Utah's conservative Jake Garn is waffling at supporting the project. And Nevada and Idaho Indian tribes are opposed to the project, which would cut through many of their lands.

The Sagebrush Rebellion

Part of the cause of the problems ranchers and farmers face in the Rockies is that decisions concerning the western environment are made by eastern politicians who believe the most absurd myths about the western landscape. The same front page of the *Minidoka County News* that reported the FARM conference discussion of the Sagebrush Rebellion also quoted Secretary of Agriculture Bob Bergland as saying he had "no personal problem" regarding a takeover of public lands in the West by local governments or private interests. "Most of the public land in the West that's being managed is, for all practical purposes, commercially worthless," said Bergland.[5]

It is exactly this belief in the myth of the "Barren Desert," this myopic ignorance, that has given rise to the Sagebrush Rebellion— the movement to bring control of western resources back to western states. Proponents of the Rebellion point out studies showing that absentee owners rarely maintain the land as well as tenant owners do and argue that the lands could be better managed by the western states themselves. Opponents of the movement, arguing that the cost of administering the arid lands would far outweigh any financial gain from controlling them, charge that the real motive behind the Rebellion is not to preserve the lands but to exploit them.

There is no doubt that foreign ownership has contributed to the degradation of western rangeland in the past. British and Welsh cattle concerns depleted large tracts of rangeland in the nineteenth century. Consequently, some experts worry about reports that for-eigners are buying U.S. agricultural land. Estimates of the farm-d owned by foreigners range from 4 to 10 million acres. Most of that is in the South (principally in Tennessee, North Carolina, and Georgia), but prime farmland is in short supply in the West, and some farmers worry that they will be forced to compete with interests who have invested in the land but do not care if they make a profit.

The Sagebrush Rebellion received much attention in the western states during the early months of 1980, when this volume was in press. Idaho's Attorney-General Leroy vowed to plead his case before the Supreme Court, arguing that the Carey Act desert lands should be reopened to homesteading. The Idaho House and Senate both passed legislation aimed at following Nevada's lead in the movement. Utah's Orrin Hatch, in a letter to editors and broadcasters, suggested that "thousands of new jobs, millions of acres of land, and billions of dollars in new profits could accrue to the people of our western states as a result of the passage" of Sagebrush Rebellion legislation.[6] The Utah legislature passed a law that, like Nevada's, would attempt to wrest control of the public lands from the federal government. In March 1980 Governor Dixie Lee Ray of Washington signed a bill meant to implement a proposed constitutional amendment which supposedly would allow the state to take over the federally owned lands within its borders. In the same month the Wyoming Senate gave final approval to a bill that would place public lands under the control of the state.

Senator James McClure of Idaho gave his support to the movement, but Senator Mark Hatfield said, "It's not impressed me enough to give it any thought."[7] Judging by the reaction of Interior Department officials, they *have* given it considerable thought. In December 1979, Bureau of Land Management Director Frank Gregg emphasized that the agency is merely a messenger for Congress, that Congress directed many of the policies that are angering westerners, and that the BLM is really interested in "good land management that will influence the whole environment that the BLM operates within." The real reason for the Rebellion was, he suggested, that Congress had ordered the range improved and wilderness areas set aside.[8]

Early in February the Interior Department seemed to begin taking a much stronger stance. Gregg contended that it has been the efforts of the agency to correct management problems that have spawned the movement—implying that some cattlemen are less interested in good management than in high profits. Assistant Interior Secretary Guy Martin flatly stated that Sagebrush Rebellion legislation is unconstitutional. Nevada, he said, has been *invited* to push its claim in the courts. Indeed, Secretary of the Interior Cecil Andrus has told Nevada it is time to put its money where its mouth has been. "Ever since the Nevada Legislature passed this so-called Sagebrush Rebellion law," Andrus said, "the state has made all sorts of excuses why it hasn't brought a court challenge." Andrus, the Interior Department, and the Justice Department are confident that the courts will not allow the states to renege on agreements, made at the time of statehood, that they would never claim any public lands within their borders.[9]

In the meantime the BLM has been emphasizing a new flexibility in range policy, a flexibility that affects the livelihoods of ranchers and farmers. Idaho Governor John Evans supported this trend, saying, "Improved federal-state partnership in land-management issues must be encouraged rather than the current effort in some states, including Idaho, to promote state control of the public domain."[10]

The stakes are high in this controversy, and rhetoric has increased. An editorial in *High Country News*, fearing the results of a backlash against westerners, pointed out that you don't go around throwing dynamite at random. Idaho state representative Bert Marley put it this way, "When you're going through a cow pasture you don't walk through it looking at the sky." He went on to warn that constitutional scholars have universally agreed that only Congress has complete power to dispose of public lands. The only challenge to that doctrine culminated in the Civil War. And one representative said that the Rebellion would have just about as much effect as a joint resolution calling for a secession from the Union.

Indian tribes reacted quickly to the Sagebrush Rebellion. The intensity of their reaction indicates that they take it very seriously. Many Indian leaders believe that the Rebellion has at its roots the same motives as do movements to terminate or abrogate Indian treaty rights and reservations. The tribes fear that Nevada and other western states would not honor special rights of Indian tribes, that these states would be poor guardians of Indian treaty rights. History supports their argument.

Undersecretary of the Interior James A. Joseph, speaking for Indian interests, said,

Though they wave the banner of local control of public lands...backers [of the Sagebrush Rebellion] represent, for the most part, a handful of narrow economic interests. Their outrage is no mystery; they have lost the ability they once had to control public land decision. They continue, of course, to have a strong voice in those decisions. But it is no stronger than they deserve, for now other interests have a strong voice too.

To the "Sagebrush Rebellion" we must respond with a renewed determination to continue involving the public as broadly as possible in making land management decisions. To the extent that the "Sagebrush Rebellion" reflects genuine and legitimate frustration over the process of federal management, we must continue to work harder to be responsive, to be good neighbors and to truly serve the public interest.

To threats to the Indian trust relationship, we must respond by ensuring that the Bureau of Indian Affairs operates with the same degree of efficiency as any other program unit with the Department of the Interior.

Lionel Boyer, President of the Affiliated Tribes of the Northwest

Indians, himself a Shoshone-Bannock, said "little consideration" had been given to Indian treaty rights by those drafting Sagebrush Rebellion legislation, and that "little consideration would be given to Indian rights if the laws are implemented." The Sho-Ban statement went on to say that the implementation of Sagebrush Rebellion philosophy would "threaten directly the survival of Tribal culture and religion," which are tied to the land and to conservation practices on the land. "Such measures will also seriously deplete or destroy important Tribal food sources at a time when nearly 40 percent of the Shoshone-Bannock are unemployed."[11] The Coeur d'Alene tribe, representatives from the Duck Valley Reservation, and the Idaho Intertribal Council also joined in opposition to the Rebellion.

Must all these problems be solved solely on the basis of the economics of the moment, the sophisticated available technology, or can decisions be reached on the basis of human values? Soil Conservation Service Executive Vice-President Neil Sampson points out that we have an ethical as well as economic responsibility to the land—this, the most productive land on earth.

And today there are many good signs: Such groups as the Small Farms Resources Network in Washington are forming to help preserve the small, independent farming community. The press is taking a growing interest in the complex environmental questions being raised about some present-day farming practices. The U.S. Department of Agriculture has launched a major campaign to conserve the nation's natural resources (under the Resources Conservation Act). New agricultural research is focusing on arid lands and drought-resistant crops. (For example, at the International Arid Lands Conference in 1979, new findings reported that saline-resistant crops could now be grown with sea water under the right conditions.) The United Nations International Conference on Appropriate Technology has shown the world that groups on every continent are working to save energy and preserve physical resources for generations to come.

Is it true that human values can have meaning to the working man and woman? Are values like this of interest to the general public? Or should decisions be made entirely on technological or economic reasoning? The people do have a right to make such choices. They can enact laws allowing counties to buy development rights from farmers; they can restrict strip-mining; they can determine to a certain extent the highest and best use for their resources; through intelligent and appropriate purchase they can encourage the existence of the family farm; and they can determine the direction and shape of their cities.

The people of the Mountain West can decide to keep a ranching/farming economy and culture. Such a decision surely will involve some sacrifice, but the alternative may be to sacrifice the West itself.

I invite you to read what the experts have to say on the future of agriculture in the Rocky Mountains and to decide for yourself what that future will be.

The Time is Now

Alvin M. Josephy, Jr.

Not very long ago—in the 1950s—in those comfortable times when the American people's principal concern was in policing the world rather than in conserving natural resources, those few individuals who called themselves "conservationists" (and who were regarded as a weird lot) used to wag their fingers nervously and warn of an approaching doomsday. Come the year 2000, they would say, we will have to face some terrible problems: There won't be food enough to go around, the water and air will be dangerously polluted, the oceans will be dead or dying, and we will be threatened by grave energy shortages. Now it is apparent that we brushed aside those warnings too casually, preferring to persuade ourselves that we had plenty of time to come to grips with them, or that when they struck sometime in the early part of the twenty-first century, we would be six feet under, having bequeathed them, like the national debt, to an unlucky future generation. But here we are now—some twenty or more years ahead of time—the surprised and unlucky generation ourselves.

Among the more profound changes that have occurred with breathtaking rapidity and which form a significant backdrop for agriculture in the West are the external pressures being visited on the United States, particularly by many nations characterized as small, nonaligned, and certainly less powerful than the United States. After years of isolationism, we emerged from the last World War with the realization that our globe after all was one world, split unfortunately into two competing ideologies and that we had the

[19]

rather clear-cut obligation to assist the small, less-developed countries and in that way keep them out of our rival's camp. Today there are a number of different camps in the world and a complexity of diverse and competing aims that have piled up bewildering financial, economic, and political problems for this country.

I would like to mention one attitude that we have not yet fully recognized but that has meaning for us today. Everyone appreciates more clearly than ever that this is one globe, but the peoples of some nations, particularly nonaligned countries, have a new perspective on the nature of the earth's wholeness as it applies to the developed, industrial nations and especially the rich, profligate people of the United States. What we used to give away freely as a good and concerned neighbor, we now owe—simply because we are fortunate enough to possess the natural resources that made fortune and power possible. We are beginning to see the evidence of this new development in the way some countries are dealing with us politically and economically. We can also see it in their perspective of our history.

It goes something like this: Five hundred years ago the Western Hemisphere was a sudden new addition to the rest of the world. Save for its use by a relatively small indigenous population, it was an unexploited storehouse of immense natural resources of almost every kind. Those who came to what is now the United States were accorded the exclusive and fortunate opportunity to appropriate and use the abundant, previously untapped riches and thus to build a mighty and wealthy nation. Cheapness and waste were hallmarks of this vast and rapid world development. But inevitably there had to be an end. And in large measure, the end—certainly the end of cheapness and waste—is now. Some of our neighbors in the world now feel that the American people are back on square one. Their peculiar advantage is now over, or is approaching its end. Our own Cedars of Lebanon, so to speak, are squandered, and we are facing the prospect of having to be on a par with the other nations of the world. If we feel that we have a right to their remaining resources, they feel that they have a right to ours—as equals. And they will talk to us, as equals, about production and consumption and almost anything else affecting the future of mankind. What some of them are now saying, in short, is, "Because of your resources, you've had it better than us for a long time. Now you've got to be like the rest of us."

In this new message are enormous short- and long-range implications for all Americans. And nowhere would this be more true than in the American West, the last large-scale repository, not only of bounteous natural resources, but also of traits and life-styles that all Americans have cherished throughout their history. Here, amid the majesty and splendors of the sprawling western landscape, many of us continue to enjoy independence, freedom, individualism, and self-reliance.

But now that life-style too seems threatened. The rest of the United States, echoing the overseas voices, seems to be focusing on the West and saying, "You have had your day. But now you've got to integrate with the rest of us, be like us. Your day of special benefits is over."

I have simplified a world view of America, and a corresponding American view of the Rocky Mountain West, to suggest that the questions that surface in the next few years will have an enormous, rapidly changing, and complicated context: the inflationary impact of rising competitive world demands, the availability to the United States of foreign energy and other vital resources, the production of food with which to pay for oil, the position of the United States vis-a-vis the communist and nonaligned nations, the international trade balances, the stability of the dollar, and so forth. In fact, the Rocky Mountain West is already under assault on a dozen fronts by forces that do not, and cannot, take into consideration any special pleading that what is here has any right any longer to remain as it is. Let us consider one example: As a consequence of our current military posture, the SALT debate, and defense arrangements, plans are under way to locate a huge MX launch complex in the Rocky Mountain West. These systems, including a need for giant road networks, would take large areas of productive land out of agriculture and would change and ruin the life-style of much of the rural West.

To those who live here, and those who visit to regain values and enjoy comforts denied them elsewhere, the prospect of such a change is dreaded. But whether or not the MX plans are implemented, change does seem inevitable. Thus, the immediate task will no doubt be to minimize destructive change and maximize protections—or, stated another way, to accommodate the pressures, using innovations and creative solutions that will retain as much of the present good as is possible.

From the start, what should be recognized is that almost every feature of the Rocky Mountain West that is treasured has existed—and continues to exist—because this region rests on a ranching/farming

Zuni gardens with their low walls, and the Zuni River after a heavy rain.
Zuni, New Mexico, 1919.

economy: wide-open spaces, unpolluted air, the bounties and beauties
of nature, the ease and grace and freedom of life. As that economy
goes, so will go the West. Therefore, agriculture is burdened with
enormous responsibilities to adjust to change.

Many of the major pressures have already been brought to bear.
Land is being overrun by developers, subdividers, and realtors, by
builders of shopping centers, highways, and lakes, by military bases
and waste-disposal sites. Other land is being withdrawn from ranching and farming for industry, recreation, and other competing uses.
Proliferating rules and regulations of state and federal bureaucracies
are inhibiting or crippling agricultural enterprises. Water is being
diverted from traditional agricultural users to nonagricultural consumers, and what is left is occasioning increased competition and
uncertainty among agriculturalists, including newly assertive
Indian tribes whose rights to adequate water were not protected
in the past.

As conflicts develop, it is hard enough to know where to put the
blame or how to identify sources of problems, much less how to cope
with them. In a piecemeal way, individuals, as well as isolated

regions, feel the special impacts. The Bureau of Reclamation, established to help the agriculturalist, is now snubbing him, turning away from him to service new and better-heeled clients, notably the huge multinational energy companies. The Bureau is taking water from the farmer and rancher and giving it to industry, not only in individual areas, but from basin to basin. Agricultural water users, with their rights still unadjudicated, have great reason to fear the future, when they may not only lose water that they thought was theirs by the rights of western water law but also see water from their basin transferred to other basins—from the Snake to the Colorado or from the Tongue to the Bighorn.

But what are the defenses against urban sprawl? Against inflation that is imperiling the family farm? Against the growing arrogance and highhanded, patronizing, absolutely rotten human relations of large numbers of field personnel of such federal agencies as the BLM and Forest Service? What are hard-pressed ranchers and farmers to make of high technology costs, new public-land policies, choices based on the highest and best use of resources, all of which seem to affect the agriculturalist adversely? And what are policymakers themselves to think of the so-called Sagebrush Rebellion?

What has so far come to pass is almost nothing when compared with what seems about to transpire. In the face of the energy crisis, certain areas of the Rocky Mountain West have begun to feel the boom impacts of rapid and chaotic industrialization and urbanization, before which ranching and farming must retreat. The huge power plants and/or strip mines at places like Rock Springs and Gillette, Wyoming, Decker and Colstrip, Montana, and Farmington and Shiprock, New Mexico, are only the faint sounds of an orchestra warming up before the crashing discordance of scores of synthetic fuel plants, coal gasification and liquefaction producers, oil-shale surface retorting facilities, new coal and uranium strip mines, processing plants, power-generating plants, new towns and industrial complexes, reservoirs, pipelines, railroad lines, slurry lines, transmission lines, highways, and service centers.

Let us consider the implications for the Rocky Mountain West of the Carter Administration's Energy Security Corporation and Energy Mobilization Board—the board appointed to direct the development of at least sixteen coal-liquefaction plants and eight oil-shale surface retorting facilities by 1990 (some industry spokesmen are suggesting as many as sixty plants by that time), the other to be given the authority to fast-track the building of energy facilities, including powers to interpret impeding state and local laws, tailor and compress certain state, local, and federal procedures and requirements, and even waive state, federal, and local laws that hold up siting and construction.

The demand for sites, immense amounts of water, rights-of-way, and other facilities for the plants and the communities that will spring up around them will have an adverse effect on agricultural land and water rights and on landowner due process. Moreover, ensuing air and water pollution, the crowding-in of new population, the overrunning of additional land areas by suburbs and recreationalists, and the abrupt change of local mores, economic standards and values, life-styles, and political and social structures will create additional problems for ranchers and farmers.

These wrenching changes have already begun. For example, certain Powder River farmers and ranchers were staggered by their treatment at the hands of Wyoming's Industrial Siting Council, which was reviewing a large coal-fired plant that would create adverse impacts on agricultural interests in Platte County. "The Council," said a follow-up report by the Power River Basin Resource Council (a landowners' group),

> glossed over... water conflicts and other ways the plant would hurt the agricultural community. Instead they reasoned that a farmer or rancher who was forced out of business or lost income because of the plant, could go to work at the plant and make more money that way. And if the plant ran out of water and went shopping for more agricultural water or infringed on a prior user, again the Council saw no problems. They noted that the agricultural water user could sell out or sue. Although agriculture is the economic backbone of Platte County (where the plant would be sited), the Council gave little consideration to its continued vitality. They wrote agriculture off, concluding that an industrial economic base created by the plant would probably improve the area's overall economic condition—a bigger tax base, higher wages, more sales. They chose not to worry about agriculture and its meager returns, and refused to even give the impact of the plant on agriculture a second look.

That report of three years ago reflects an event and an attitude that is bound to become increasingly familiar in the agricultural

West. At the same time, we all know that the production of food must continue in this region. But because the farmer and the rancher must have adequate land, water, and energy, the increased competition for those resources will inevitably require that they make innovative adjustments and changes. They will have to maintain the land's productivity and conserve water and energy as never before, probably by new methods of production and transportation. And any government that wishes to maintain food production will have to resist the natural tendency to favor a utility or energy company, which can pay more for land and resources than a farmer or rancher. The surest way to add a food crisis to an energy crisis is to assert—as did a Carter Administration task force in 1977: "In the most simple terms, the fact is that the price utility and other major coal users are willing to pay for the resource will normally far exceed the long-term income potential of a given plot of land for agricultural production"—and then to encourage exploitation of the resource.

Wheat Field, Ojo Caliente. Zuni Reservation, New Mexico, 1919.

This brief reflection on some difficult problems facing agriculture in the Rocky Mountain West should not at all ring with defeatism. The first signs of these problems are appearing all around us, and we know that they will accelerate and multiply. It is time, here and now, to identify them and get to know their causes as well as their manifestations clearly and completely—and to do so quickly. If this is a region of individualism and extreme privacy, it may be apt to begin thinking more of cooperation and organization, as have the landowners in eastern Montana, Wyoming, and the western Dakotas. The plants and facilities of industrialization will come cascading into the Rocky Mountain West, and so too will people—tens and hundreds of thousands of newcomers, creating not only new towns, but also vast political and sociological changes, few of which will accord respect to the individualism and privacy that now exist.

You of the West are here now. The newcomers are not. The time is now to get ready for them. Otherwise they will chart the future of the Rocky Mountain West, including its agriculture.

The Future Breeding of Cowboys and Ranchers

"Hey May," Sally Jane says to her teen-age daughter,
    "Why don't you put on your pretty red dress
and go out dancin' with that highschool boy John Smith,
    when he asks you out of an evening?"

"I don't want to go dancin' with that boy, Moma,"
        May says to Sally Jane.
    He's handsome, and he's nice,
            but when I go to the town dancin' there,
I'll fix my hair, and wear that red dress.
    I'll be dancin' with a rancher, or a cowboy."

    "Ah," says Sally Jane,
        "There may be some hope for us after all."

Drum Hadley

Part One
Physical Resources

K. Ross Toole is Hammond Professor of Western History in the University of Montana. He has been Director of the Montana Historical Society, the Museum of the City of New York, and the Museum of New Mexico. His latest book is *The Rape of the Great Plains; Northwest America, Cattle and Coal.*

C. C. Gordon is Professor of Botany and Director of the Environmental Studies Laboratory at the University of Montana. He is a member of the Board of Trustees of the Environmental Defense Fund and of the Federal Energy Administration Environmental Advisory Committee.

Neil Sampson is Executive Vice President of the National Association of Conservation Districts. He is the author of several articles and essays on land-use planning and conservation.

The Energy Crisis and the Northern Great Plains

K. Ross Toole

In a recent issue of the *Saturday Review* dedicated largely to corporate communications, one section deals with corporate problems under the heading "Corporate America is making every effort to dispel lingering public distrust and suspicion." Indeed it is, but the distrust and suspicion are not "lingering"; rather, they are widespread and very active. Witness last spring's polls indicating that more than half the American people believed that the gasoline shortages and price escalations were deliberate ploys by the major oil companies to make obscene profits. Of course, there was little to substantiate the charge. The point is that more than half the American people believe the charge to be true.

The danger in this kind of attitude is that American corporations may well lose a vital constituency, namely, the American people. I suppose I am a case in point. I am—or was—a middle-of-the-road Democrat who happened to believe that regardless of its faults the free-enterprise system is the best economic system yet invented by man. But I can believe that only if the system remains both free and enterprising. I now harbor serious doubts on that score. Moreover, I do not believe that government regulations can *ever* work as efficiently as the marketplace. But that is true only if corporate America is kept from sabotaging that marketplace.

In that connection, back to the voice of corporate America: "Government regulations are strangling us; deregulate us, and we will put all our profits into solving the energy crisis." And as a corollary, "We have a critical energy problem [no thoughtful Ameri-

[31]

can disagrees with that], but our capacity for attacking the problem is completely debilitated by environmental regulations." For that last assertion, read, "We are frustrated by eagle freaks, daisy pickers, and the worshipers of three-inch fish."

And there the line is drawn: All will be well if the business of America remains business and the kooks and the flaky individuals are given no recourse in the law of the land—federal, state, or local. The argument is appealing because of its utter simplicity. The trouble is that the source of difficulty—the energy shortage—is almost infinitely complex, and nothing renders it more complex than the assertion by corporate energy conglomerates that the only barriers between America and economic Nirvana are government and environmental nonsense.

Well, all this was settled, of course, by President Carter's pietistic speech on energy in the spring of 1979. What we have here it seems, is not really an energy problem at all. It is a crisis of the American spirit—a crisis of the American people's confidence in themselves. It is my own subjective view that this probably came as something of a surprise to the American people, who hadn't been brooding too much about their spirit but had been brooding a good deal about a nonexistent federal energy policy.

In one basic respect the energy crisis confronts us with an awesome dilemma—or it seems to: How much productive land, how much clean water, and how much pure air must we trade off to become energy self-sufficient? The *political* answer now seems very clear: "As much as we have to and as fast as we can." However, if the question were framed differently, the political answer might be less appealing. The real question is this: "How much food and fiber and how much human health must we trade for energy self-sufficiency?" Now the political answer carries considerably less appeal. After all, hunger is an even nastier specter than gasoline lines.

But is the question really legitimate? Does present energy policy really threaten our food, fiber, and health? Are land, water, and air really in jeopardy? Do we not, in fact, have plenty of reserves, plenty of leeway, for a reasonable tradeoff? That is the nub of the question and the core of the real debate. My own answer (and I have a lot of company) is that we have very little reserve, that a reasonable tradeoff is *not* involved here, that in choosing current policy we have almost locked the door on right policies. (And I am convinced that there are ways to achieve energy sufficiency.) I would further assert that it is very, very late.

Of course the problem is national and international, and in confining my remarks to the northern Great Plains I do not intend to parochialize the issue. It is simply that one has to start somewhere—and this is a useful kind of paradigm.

The proposed synfuel program aside, power companies have been busily constructing enormous mine-mouth coal-fired generating plants on the western rim of the Great Plains for more than a decade. However, the high winds move from west to east on those plains. And these plants, sophisticated scrubbers notwithstanding, produce large quantities of microscopic sulfur particles as well as nitrogen oxides that rise high into the atmosphere. Here, mingling with air and water, they are converted into nitric and sulfuric acids. Sulfuric acid, even in very dilute form, is very nasty stuff. Most of us remember the ditty from high school chemistry class:

> Poor little Johnny isn't anymore.
> What he thought was H_2O was H_2SO_4.

Acid rainfall is no new phenomenon. It has been around for a very long time in the eastern United States. And it has been a serious problem in parts of Europe. For example, the Norwegian Ministry of the Environment estimates that its salmon industry today is only 2 percent of what it was in 1885, the cause of the decline being acid precipitation. The Norwegian Mininstry of the Environment makes no bones about the connection between acid rainfall and both immediate and chronic health problems, including "respiratory ailments, cancer, and heart and vascular disease."[1]

The effect of acid rainfall (or simply the deposition of dry sulfur on soil) is chemically complicated. Suffice it to say that the pH of the soil (its acidity or alkalinity) is changed—*and the change is permanent.* Chronic or acute nitrogen deficiency occurs, with the result that yields decrease and crude fiber and low-protein stocks increase, sometimes rather dramatically.

The severity of the effects and the size of the area affected depend of course on the size of the power plants, the velocity of the wind, and the chemical variables in the upper atmosphere. However, these Brobdingnagian plants now built or under frantic construction will deposit acid precipitation or dry depositions across the breadbasket of America. If the synfuels program actually becomes operative in the coal-bearing sections of the northern Great Plains, the effect on the lush farmlands to the east will be catastrophic. Svante Oden, a deeply concerned Swedish scientist, wrote,

If one permits the effects of humans on the environment to go too far, it will not be within human capacity to have any effect on the reaction on the part of nature. In other words, the continuing emission of sulfur into the atmosphere can result in very high acidification in years to come irrespective of whether or not the sulfur emission is completely halted during those years.[2]

If the atmosphere and agricultural lands are thus under assault, water is no less in jeopardy. Acid rainfall or dry deposition acidifies water, rendering it sterile.

Water and land are utterly inseparable; therefore, the threat to one constitutes a threat to the other. And in the northern Great Plains there are two threats: strip mining and *in situ* uranium mining. Unfortunately, little solid research has been done on the effects of strip mining on subsurface water. And because in situ uranium mining is a new process, research on its groundwater implications is nascent. What happens beneath the earth is complex, and in complexity lies trouble: It is terribly difficult to cry danger without definitive research. But there *is* research, and none of it is comforting.

Strip mining first: In southern Saskatchewan, southeastern Montana, western North Dakota, and northeastern Wyoming (the Fort Union Coal Formation), coal seams are the aquifer; the groundwater is contained and, indeed, purified by the coal seams. If that aquifer is broken by strip mining at the *low* point of any given groundwater basin, the water flows into the abyss. If that occurs, surrounding wells go dry and the water table falls so that it can no longer reach the roots of grasses or crops. The problem, however, resides in the fact that we simply don't know enough about the subsurface geology of this huge area to be able to pinpoint the critical areas. It is *not* sufficient merely to exempt the alluvial valleys.

What we do know, primarily from the research of Wayne Van Voast of the Montana Bureau of Mines and the National Academy of Sciences, is frightening.[3] We run the risk (albeit how much risk we do not know) of drying up productive range and cropland covering an extensive area around the site of a strip-mining operation.

In situ uranium mining, which is well under way in Texas, Colorado, and Wyoming and is beginning in Montana, poses all kinds of potential hazards. Interestingly, but not surprisingly, spokesmen for Westinghouse, Mobil Oil, and others hail the development of in situ uranium mining as environmentally sound. There are, they say, no scars created upon the land, no solid-waste disposal problem, no necessity for expensive reclamation. In those claims they are quite right. But the impact on groundwater is quite another matter.

In situ mining is a simple process. Holes are drilled to a depth often exceeding 400 feet. A chemical leaching agent, usually ammonia and hydrogen peroxide, is then pumped in huge quantities down the holes. The chemicals scour the sandstone and separate from it the loosely bonded uranium particles. Then the liquid solution— or at least some of it—is pumped back to the surface. Finally, the uranium is extracted, dried, and shipped in the form of "yellow cake" to enrichment plants in the East.

However, there are two very serious drawbacks to this system. As in strip mining, the aquifer can readily be broken with a concomitant drop in the level of groundwater. Worse, the chemical solution in many instances has been shown to "migrate" far beyond the site of its introduction. Ammonia in particular is highly toxic. It kills fish in a solution of only 0.2 parts per million. Though there is argument about its toxicity to humans, it is well known that ammonia-polluted water causes a disease called methemoglobinemia, often fatal. The Environmental Protection Agency has reported that about two thousand infants have contracted this disease although no in situ mining cases have thus far been reported. We simply don't know yet what level of ammonia is toxic to humans, and the EPA has set no federal ammonia standards for drinking water. All we know is that ammonia is toxic and that thousands and thousands of gallons of it are now being pumped into underground water all over the West. We know that it can migrate, but we do not know how far it can migrate or what damage, aside from polluting drinking water, the chemical soup may ultimately cause. It is a fair assumption that plant life will not take kindly to ammonia and hydrogen peroxide.

Because in situ uranium mining is almost infinitely cheaper than any other technique, we know one more thing: In full cry the energy conglomerates are attacking the critics of in situ mining— asserting in Wyoming, for instance, that "a jar of pickle relish is richer in ammonia than the water from our mines." Again, those who want more research before we pump billions of gallons of toxic chemicals into the underground water system of the northern Great Plains are called "alarmists," "daisy pickers," and "eagle freaks."[4]

At the very core of what is now confronting the Rocky Mountain and Plains West is the concept of the "national sacrifice area," a concept whose most egregious oversight is that the area destroyed will expand as surely as a virulent cancer will metastasize. You cannot stop the air from moving where it will move, and water will flow to the sea.

I do not for a moment assert that the coal-rich western states should lock up their resources even if they could. I do not for a moment deny that we are "a part of the main" and that our resources must now be used—and *should* be used. Nor indeed do I deny that the wise and judicious use of these resources will be of great value to the United States and even to the West.

What I do assert is that the method of utilizing these resources is wrong. What I assert is that once again a historical anomaly is operating: The East, the Congress, the federal administrators do not understand the semiarid West; they do not understand the water or live upon the land. Ask the Indian people. And that ignorance hurts not only the West but the whole nation—indeed, the world.

Robert Fulton would feel fully at home in the antediluvian coal-fired generating plants we are now frantically building. We are, presumably, the most technologically advanced nation on earth. Why is it, then, that on the long list of American industries, investor-owned utilities are at the very bottom when it comes to expenditures on research and development? They spend less than 0.25 percent of their revenues on research and development.

Magnetohydrodynamics may prove to be a pollution-free system for generating electricity from coal. Fluidized-bed combustion systems may prove to be equally pollution free. These things I don't know. What I do know is that neither private industry nor government has spent enough on either system to give us answers. And that, I think, is inexcusable.

Now comes the administration with synfuels and the Energy Mobilization Board. And without further ado, some nut (who has to be taken very seriously) marks off ten eastern Montana counties in which to place *thirty-six* huge synfuel plants! Don't they know that the water isn't there? Apparently not. Don't they know that we need the corn growing in Iowa and the wheat and other grains in Nebraska?

The proposed Energy Mobilization Board (if it comes into being as already passed by the Senate) wipes out the tenth amendment to the Constitution of the United States,[5] fundamentally undermines the federal system, and wipes off the books the environmental legis-

lation so laboriously wrought by the states—particularly the belea-
guered western states.

This pietistic man has cried havoc and let loose the dogs of
devastation. If the struggle for energy self-sufficiency is the "moral
equivalent of war," why are we killing off our own soldiers? *Most*
existing environmental legislation is designed to protect the West's
principal industry—agriculture. And that industry is no more vital
to the West than to America.

But the most distressing thing about our present policy (or lack
of policy) for attaining energy self-sufficiency is the fact that we are
doing least in the area of greatest potential. That, of course, is in the
area of conservation. In truth, we have made little progress since
"win" buttons.

Here we are, completely subject to the whims of a most
whimsical people, OPEC, and our government tells us to turn down
our thermostats and obey the speed limit. In the spring of 1980 we
we will face a 5 percent shortfall in gasoline—a shortfall that could
cause economic chaos. Our entire economy is hanging on a thread
that can be cut at a moment's notice by a fanatic in Iran or a
belligerent crackpot in Iraq. And the best our government can do is
tell us to drive more slowly.

Even if the synfuels program *were* successful (a very dubious
proposition), it could do little to alleviate our terribly dangerous
problems before the year 2000. I seriously doubt that we have that
kind of time.

Stern conservation, and *only* conservation, can put a fast dent
in the armor of our enemy. Thus, the burden of adaptation is not one
that should be borne solely by the Rocky Mountain West; it is a burden to be borne by America. A wrong national policy emanating from
Washington is simply *not* a policy to which we should adapt in
the West.

We need to ration gasoline, and we need to ration it *now*. We
need to tax energy waste heavily and on a rapidly escalating scale.
We tax land according to its use. It is incorrect to say that we cannot
tax air and water according to *their* uses.

If that sounds draconian, we had better remember that the
alternative is economic chaos.

It is easy to call the American people energy gluttons because
we are. But it is fruitless to blame our problems on crises of the
American spirit or to assert that Americans have lost all confidence

in themselves. And it is even less constructive to assert that the West must go down the drain to serve the interests of international comity.

We are a young country. But time and again we have risen to meet a critical need. Nothing has changed about that in the American character. Nothing has changed about it at all.

The American people are perfectly ready to do what they have to do. That is something the politicians and the corporations had better come to understand. But if the American people are prepared *not* to do business as usual, Exxon should be prepared *not* to do business as usual. Politicians had better get their heads out of the sand—and quickly. And we in the West should give up *nothing* until something makes sense.

Coal-fired Power Plants in the Northern Great Plains and Rockies

C. C. Gordon

Because of increasing emphasis on national energy independence during the past decade, a scenario in which coal-fired power plants begin operations throughout the northern Great Plains and northern Rocky Mountain states threatens to become a reality in the very near future. Four facets of the siting of coal-fired power plants in the agricultural lands of these areas and the legislation needed to control this potential exploitation should be evaluated. They are: (1) the reasons coal-fired power plants are being sited in agricultural lands, (2) the real and potential biological impacts of the gaseous and particulate emissions of coal-fired power plants, (3) the protection afforded agricultural crops and animals by current federal and state ambient air-pollution standards, and (4) the alternative siting areas for coal-fired power plants.

Siting Coal-Fired Power Plants in Agricultural Lands

The managers of utility companies state that power plants should be sited in the northern Great Plains because it is more economical to utilize coal near the coal mines and transport electricity over transmission lines than to transport the coal to generation facilities in the large urban and industrialized load centers. Despite this argument, many coal-fired power plants are currently being sited in agricultural areas of states which have no substantial deposits and thus must depend on coal shipped in from the northern Great Plains. For example, there were tentative plans to ship Wyoming coal to proposed power plants in the agricultural areas of Orchard,

[39]

Idaho (south of Boise), and Sutherland, Nebraska (along the Platte River). And California Pacific Gas and Electric Fossil has proposed two power plants in northern California to burn coal from Utah for load centers in San Francisco and Oakland.

Why are coal-fired power plants being sited in our agricultural areas rather than in the urban and industrialized load centers? My answers to that question are:

1. The utility companies receive less public harassment by siting in sparsely populated areas.

2. When air-pollution damage to vegetation does occur, it goes unnoticed or is nonquantifiable.

3. The state and federal air-quality agencies do less monitoring of stationary sources of air-pollution located in rural areas than of those in urban areas because of these agencies' emphasis on damage to human health as opposed to vegetation impacts.

4. When and if agricultural crops are seriously damaged by air-pollution, it costs less to pay for these damages than to face an irate public in large urban areas.

Real and Potential Biological Impacts of Gaseous and Particulate Emissions of Coal-Fired Power Plants

Vegetation can scavenge a large percentage of the gaseous and particulate emissions released by coal-fired power plants. However, sensitive plant species can be severely damaged when the ambient concentrations of gaseous pollutants such as sulfur dioxide and nitrogen dioxide are substantially above normal—that is, equal to or above federal ambient air standards—for several days. This is known as acute air-pollution damage and is usually fairly easy to diagnose. Although acute damage to vegetation has been found around some of the coal-fired power plants in the eastern United States, it has not been reported in the western states. The most common type of crop and vegetation injury found near large stationary sources of air pollution is chronic damage which is extremely difficult for both agriculturalists and air-pollution scientists to detect and quantify.

During the last five years, a series of studies by several federal and university laboratories in the cattle grazing and forested areas of southeastern Montana have demonstrated that the impacts of sulfur dioxide upon the native vegetation and insects are slow and insidious but could have serious long-term consequences to agriculture.

Unfortunately, these long-term impacts cannot be quantified throughout the northern Great Plains and northern Rocky Mountain states unless intensive field studies are conducted in these areas before large stationary sources of air pollution such as coal-fired power plants are sited and begin operations.

Currently, no western states require these types of studies to determine the normal health and growth patterns of those species of flora and fauna which have sustained farming and ranching of these areas. Without these presiting biological studies, there will be no means for anyone to quantify any chronic air pollution damage to the agricultural lands after the power plants are sited there.

Current Federal and State Ambient Air-Pollution Standards for the Protection of Agricultural Crops and Animals

There are state and federal ambient air-pollution standards regulating most of the gaseous pollutants released by coal-fired power plants. These standards were established by the regulatory agencies after months and years of bitter debate. In general, the battle was won by industries at both the federal and state levels. If the legally allowable ambient concentrations of SO_x, NO_x, O_3, and HF were actually present in the arid regions of the northern Great Plains and northern Rocky Mountain states 20 to 30 percent of the time during the growing season, farming and ranching would no longer be possible or profitable in these areas. Luckily, these kinds of concentrations are rarely seen, even around some of the worst polluting stationary sources in the western states, such as Anaconda copper smelter in Montana, Bunker Hill smelters in Idaho, and the Garfield copper smelter in Utah.

My basic point here is that there are currently no federal or state ambient air standards to adequately protect vegetation and animals from many gases and trace elements released by industrial sources. Thus, even when utility companies claim that the emissions from the proposed power plants in agricultural areas will meet all federal and state regulations, there is no assurance that the agricultural crops and animals will not be damaged.

Alternative Siting Areas for Coal-Fired Power Plants

There are two very viable alternatives to siting coal-fired power plants in agricultural areas. The first is to site them at the load centers in the large urban or industrialized areas where the best available pollution control technology undoubtedly would be required. More important, however, is that waste heat from power plants in urban areas could be used by other industries, commerce, and even for home heating. In Europe, approximately 25 percent of the waste heat of power plants is utilized. Because of our fast-dwindling coal resources, it behooves us to utilize this large remaining fossil resource with much more respect than we have.

Other benefits of siting power plants in urban areas are less sociological disruption, fewer transmission corridors across agricultural lands, and more dependable service to the populated urban areas.

The second alternative to coal-fired power plants in the large agricultural areas is the sacrifice area, or the planned industrial complex. This complex is utilized in the state of Maryland where the power plant siting protocol calls for the regulatory state agency to select those areas in the state where the least biological and sociological impacts will occur. These parcels of land are then sold to the utility companies when they decide they need to increase their generating capacity.

In the northern Rocky Mountain states, sacrifice areas would not be too difficult to select, although local residents would not be pleased in many cases. Ideal sacrifice areas would be hilly or mountainous areas with abundant vegetation which can be easily regenerated at little to nominal cost. The vegetation would be an excellent scavenger of pollutants from the power plants, and pollutants such as SO_x and NO_x would not be allowed to remain in the atmosphere to form sulfuric or nitric acids. While the scavenging vegetation can and probably would occasionally be damaged or destroyed by the emissions, this vegetation would be replaced with new plants, and the long-term costs would be less than allowing widespread damage by these gases and particulates.

The Quantity and Quality of Farmland in the Rocky Mountain Region

Neil Sampson

The future of agriculture in the Rocky Mountain Region is dependent, as it is in the rest of the nation (and the world), on the quantity and quality of land and water. All projections about the future of agriculture are relevant only to the extent that they take into account real limitations in those resources. Those real limits are the controlling factor. And in the Rocky Mountain Region the controlling factor is irrigation water. *In this region, as in perhaps no other, supplemental water is the key to agricultural productivity.*

That fact affords no particular comfort as one views the future. Irrigated agricultures have always been fragile. The early Egyptians had amazingly sophisticated irrigation systems, but those and the Mesopotamian systems failed. They failed, not because of a lack of water or of skill in its management, but because of overgrazing in the mountain watersheds. Initially that overgrazing led to soil erosion, flash flooding, excess sediment in the water; ultimately it destroyed both the mountain-land productivity and the irrigated agriculture in the valleys.

Today sediment and salt pollution are of only peripheral interest to "practical" people concerned with economic growth and agricultural productivity. But to those ancient peoples, soil erosion and water pollution meant the end of agriculture and their economy. Thus as we look at present trends affecting the land and water of the Rocky Mountain Region, we might very well ask whether we are heading for the same type of problem.

[43]

Several national studies that are under way give insight into the quantity and quality of land and water for agriculture in the Rocky Mountains. These have generated a great deal of statistical data. What this data shows will be familiar to most of you who are familiar with the Mountain West, but facts and figures may be of some value in explaining this vast and often misunderstood region to other folks around the country.

From the standpoint of land resources, the Mountain Region is a hardship case. In addition to the fact that much of the land is in federal ownership, the land that is not federally owned is largely marginal for agricultural production. Consider a few facts, looking first at the capability of the land to sustain continuous agriculture as reflected by the Soil Conservation Service's Land Capability Classification System.[1]

In this system, land is classified according to its suitability for cultivated agriculture. Class I land can be intensively farmed without hazard, Class II needs moderate conservation treatment in order to be safely farmed, and Class III needs fairly intensive conservation care to prevent permanent land damage. Class IV land is marginal and can be cultivated safely only with intensive conservation treatment, while Classes V through VIII are progressively less suited to any type of cultivation.

For the nation as a whole, almost half (43 percent) of the nonfederal lands fall in Capability Classes I to III. For the mountain Region, the percentage is only 18. We have an additional 13 percent in Class IV, but the overwhelming proportion of the nonfederal land —some 70 percent—is in Classes VI through VIII.

Stated another way, even though the Mountain Region has roughly 20 percent of the nation's nonfederal land, it has only 3 percent of the Nation's Class I land, 3 percent of the supply of Class II land, and 13 percent of the Class III land. The availability of high-quality agricultural land is a limiting factor for agriculture in this region and will remain so.

Another way to look at the nonfederal land resources of the region is to evaluate the supply of prime farmland. The U.S. Department of Agriculture defines prime farmland as land that has the best combination of physical and chemical characteristics for producing food, feed, forage, fiber, and oilseed crops. To be classified as prime farmland, the land must meet technical criteria and be available for agriculture. That is, it must not be permanently committed to a nonagricultural use such as urban development.[2]

Table 1. Nonfederal Rural Land in 1977, by Land-Capability Class and by State, Mountain Region (in thousands of acres)

State	I	II	III	IV	V	VI	VII–VIII	Total
Arizona	768	252	301	245	0	19,655	18,443	39,664
Colorado	149	2,175	5,264	10,475	265	12,644	10,324	41,296
Idaho	127	2,208	3,359	2,835	174	4,221	5,863	18,787
Montana	0	1,231	23,231	10,712	165	19,108	10,181	64,628
Nevada	0	569	544	229	86	1,940	6,916	10,284
New Mexico	206	785	2,048	2,648	80	15,437	29,064	50,268
Utah	42	652	932	931	63	2,192	11,025	15,837
Wyoming	12	670	3,019	4,924	117	12,176	11,103	32,021
Regional Total	1,304	8,542	38,698	32,999	950	87,373	102,919	272,785
Regional Percent	0.5	3	14	12	0.5	32	38	100
National Total	38,303	287,338	287,888	188,591	29,259	266,600	303,499	1,404,483
National Percent	3	20	20	13	2	19	23	100
Region as Percentage of Nation	3	3	13	17	3	33	34	19.4

Source. United States Department of Agriculture, Soil Conservation Service, "1977 SCS National Resource Inventories," Unpublished Report, 1978.

One important criterion that prime farmland must satisfy is that it have moisture adequate to grow crops in seven or more years out of ten. In general, this means that, unless an area has an average annual rainfall of around twenty inches, even its best soils will not qualify as prime farmland without supplemental irrigation. And in the Mountain Region most land producing crops with the required regularity needs irrigation.

The farmers of the Mountain Region are already farming most of the prime farmland. Nearly two-thirds of it is in irrigated cropland, and only 21 percent is in pasture and range or "other" use. There may be other acres, either in private or federal ownership, where the addition of irrigation water would qualify the soil for designation as prime farmland, but we have no data that would give us that estimate.

In terms of irrigated cropland, this region has its share of the prime land. As we noted earlier, the Mountain Region contains about 20 percent of the nonfederal land in the nation, and Table 2 shows that it also contains 20 percent of the prime farmland cur-

Table 2. Prime Farmland in 1977, by Current Use, Mountain Region (in thousands of acres)

State	Cropland Irrigated	Cropland Nonirrigated	Pasture & Range	Forest	Other	Total
Arizona	1,086	1	31	0	45	1,163
Colorado	1,260	354	103	0	42	1,759
Idaho	2,407	582	450	5	64	3,508
Montana	501	385	300	3	48	1,237
Nevada	245	0	45	0	15	305
New Mexico	494	3	14	0	5	516
Utah	659	15	33	0	10	717
Wyoming	226	517	1,127	0	19	1,889
Regional Total	6,878	1,857	2,103	8	248	11,094
Regional Percent	62	17	19	0	2	100
National Total	34,234	196,397	62,785	42,370	10,712	346,498
National Percent	10	57	18	12	3	100
Region as Percentage of Nation	20	1	3	0	2	3.2

Source.   USDA, SCS, "1977 National Resource Inventories."

rently being cropped. Where the region is limited is in prime farmland that can be dry-farmed. Only 1 percent of the national inventory of nonirrigated cropland of prime farmland quality is found in the Mountain Region. Most of that is in Idaho, largely in the northern panhandle.

Some of the cropland in the northern part of the region and at the higher elevations was created by clearing forest lands. Table 2 indicates that while there may still be forest land in the region that can be cleared for cropland, it is not high-quality land and will not meet the criteria for prime farmland after it has been converted. This, plus the increasingly high value of forest products and the high cost of land clearing, suggests that the clearing of forest land for new cropland will be very minor. Thus, the regional picture is very different from the results of the national survey, which shows that 12 percent of the nation's supply of prime farmland is still in forest use.

From all this data, the conclusions that emerge are: (1) The Mountain Region has a limited supply of high-quality cropland, most of which is already being used for irrigated agriculture; (2) further additions to the cropland base (at least for high-quality cropland) will have to come through new irrigation; and (3) most of the best nonfederal land for new irrigation is in Idano, Montana, and Wyoming, with Wyoming having by far the greatest amount, more than 1.5 million acres. In that state, water limits may be more important than land limits, but in the rest of the region, land is, or soon will be, a limiting factor.

One way to estimate the future of land use is to look at the immediate past. In the Mountain Region, as in the rest of the nation, there has been a great deal of land-use change over the past decade. Table 3 shows, on a state-by-state basis, what has been happening and how it relates to the nation as a whole.

Cropland has remained virtually the same for the past ten years. There were about 42.5 million acres of cropland in 1967 and 42.2 million acres in 1977, but they were not the same acres. The 1977 survey doesn't tell us how many acres moved from one land use to another, so we don't know for sure what happened in that period. However, an earlier survey, completed in 1975 by the Soil Conservation Service (SCS), did show this movement, and the estimates for the Mountain Region are shown in Figure 1. This indicates that, while the total cropland acreage remained about the same over the eight-year study, about 6 million acres were taken out of cropland (mostly in conversions to pasture or range), and a different 6 million acres were added to the cropland supply (coming mostly from pasture and range land). Thus, although the cropland total remained constant, 12 million acres of land—more than 25 percent of the cropland—changed use in the eight-year period. This illustrates both the dynamics of land use and the manner in which statistics can sometimes hide important factors.

Another important shift over the past decade has been the continued expansion of irrigation. Irrigated cropland has increased by 17 percent in the region; dry cropland has declined 10 percent. The decline in dry cropland matches what has been happening in the nation, but the increase in irrigation does not. Nationally, irrigated cropland increased by about 30 percent in the past ten years, almost twice as fast as the rate of increase in the Mountain Region. Table 4 shows these estimates.

The major activity in new irrigation over the past decade has been in the Midwest and in the south-central states, as well as in parts of the East. Additions to the historically irrigated regions have

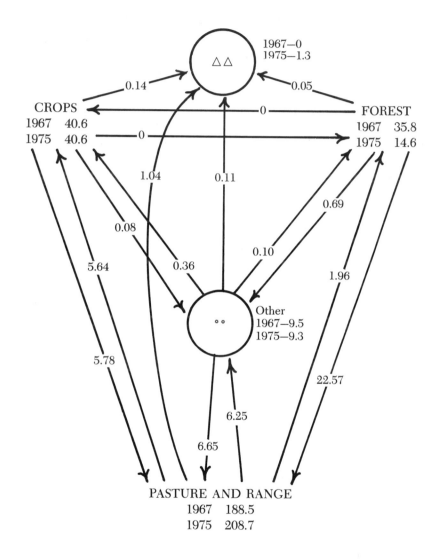

CROPS
1967   40.6
1975   40.6

FOREST
1967   35.8
1975   14.6

Other
1967—9.5
1975—9.3

PASTURE AND RANGE
1967   188.5
1975   208.7

Idle land, rural residence, etc.°°
Water and urban build-up since 1967 △△

Figure 1.
Land-use Conversions between 1967 and 1975 in the Mountain Region
(in millions of acres).

Table 3. Land-Use Trends on Nonfederal Land, 1967-77, Mountain Region (in thousands of acres)

State	Cropland			Pasture & Range			Forest			Other		
	1967	1977	Change (%)	1967	1977	Change (%)	1967	1977	Change (%)	1967	1977	Change (%)
Arizona	1,497	1,311	–12	25,320	35,103	+39	9,775	1,804	–82	2,884	1,610	– 44
Colorado	11,786	11,088	– 6	22,645	25,403	+12	6,964	3,343	–52	1,012	2,194	+117
Idaho	5,983	6,281	+ 5	7,949	7,700	– 3	4,321	4,229	– 2	323	872	+170
Montana	14,989	15,358	+ 2	43,005	41,484	– 4	7,004	6,343	– 9	520	2,415	+364
Nevada	603	1,112	+84	7,235	7,648	+ 6	409	229	–44	1,133	1,421	+ 25
New Mexico	2,617	2,275	–13	37,520	42,481	+13	9,276	3,426	–63	658	2,473	+276
Utah	2,155	1,815	–16	9,027	9,989	+11	4,665	1,066	–77	1,032	3,158	+206
Wyoming	3,044	2,967	– 3	27,329	26,904	– 2	1,554	1,163	–25	225	1,397	+521
Regional Totals	42,579	42,207	– 1	180,030	196,712	+ 9	43,968	21,603	–51	7,787	15,540	+100
National Totals	437,579	413,169	– 6	481,685	541,406	+12	460,712	369,700	–20	55,654		
Region as Percentage of Nation	9.8	10.2		37.4	36.3		9.5	5.8		14		

Sources. United States Department of Agriculture, *National Inventory of Soil and Water Conservation Needs, 1967*, Statistical Bulletin 461 (Washington, D.C., 1971); USDA Soil Conservation Service "1977 SCS National Resource Inventories," Unpublished Report, 1978.

been slower. This may be the result of land constraints, particularly the difficulty in developing federal lands, but it is more likely the result of limited water supplies and the rising cost of developing the more marginal water supplies that remain in much of the Mountain Region.

Table 4.   Changes in Cropland Use, 1967-77, Mountain Region (in thousands of acres)

State	Irrigated Cropland			Dry Cropland		
	1967	1977	Change (%)	1967	1977	Change (%)
Arizona	1,051	1,276	+21	446	35	− 92
Colorado	3,083	3,487	+13	8,703	7,601	− 13
Idaho	2,941	3,617	+23	3,042	2,664	− 12
Montana	1,648	2,262	+37	13,341	13,096	− 2
Nevada	599	1,112	+86	4	0	−100
New Mexico	1,098	1,440	+31	1,519	835	− 45
Utah	1,349	1,250	− 7	806	565	− 30
Wyoming	1,932	1,652	−15	1,112	1,315	+ 18
Regional Totals	13,701	16,096	+17	28,973	26,111	− 10
National Totals	44,255	57,647	+30	393,328	355,520	− 10
Region as Percentage of Nation	31	28	− 3	7.4	7.3	− .1

Sources.   USDA, *Inventory of Soil and Water Conservation Needs.* USDA, SCS, "1977 National Resource Inventories."

Irrigation is the mainstay of Mountain agriculture. More than 38 percent of the Mountain Region's cropland acres were irrigated in 1977, as compared with only 14 percent for the nation. That 38 percent of the cropland produced an estimated 63 percent of the dollar value of the farm crops sold in 1974.[3] Table 5 shows these data for each state in the region.

It goes without saying, then, that the future of agriculture in the region is tied tightly to the future of irrigation. But evaluating that future is very difficult because there are so many unknown factors that affect water. However, many of the factors appear negative. Figure 2 indicates the regions of the nation where overdraft of groundwater is a problem. This shows serious problems in the southern part of the Mountain Region. Figure 3, which indicates where surface-water supplies are limited, shows that the problem exists throughout most of the southern Mountain Region.

Political controversies over water rights, interbasin transfers, and new dam projects forecast problems with any new water developments. The President's new water policy stresses water conservation, and there is much benefit to be gained from such efforts in the Mountain West. But water conservation doesn't create new water, and in those areas where the available supply is being used and reused for the full length of the stream, there would be little new land irrigated even if maximum water-conservation techniques were instituted.

Water quality is a problem as well, particularly in regard to salinity. Much irrigation water in the Mountain Region contains so much salt that improper irrigation techniques can increase salinization on valuable irrigated land.[4] Preventing this from becoming a serious problem concerns conservationists and irrigators alike.

Energy costs also affect water availability. Much of the new irrigation in the past decade has come from pumped water lifted from wells or river canyons. But as the costs of electricity and natural gas have increased, the cost of pumping water from deep wells or canyons has been getting higher and higher. Only a strong agricultural economy can justify these pumping costs, and it is likely that some irrigation will not survive the next period of depressed farm prices.

Table 5. Value of Agricultural Products Sold in 1974, Mountain Region (in thousands of dollars)

State	All Agricultural Products Sold	Product from Irrigated Cropland
Arizona	491,046	488,195
Colorado	681,096	328,943
Idaho	874,989	599,226
Montana	551,584	166,026
Nevada	42,985	42,790
New Mexico	154,111	137,044
Utah	91,582	62,210
Wyoming	121,633	80,549
Regional Totals	3,009,026	1,904,983

Source. United States Census Bureau, *1974 Census of Agriculture*, vol. 2, part 9 (Washington, D.C., 1975).

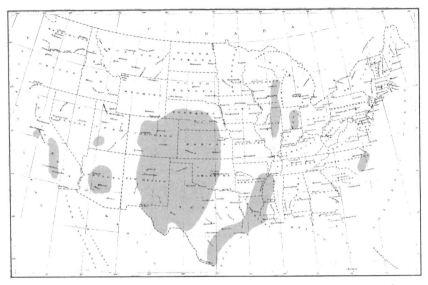

Figure 2. Overdraft of Groundwater   Areas where groundwater
                                                 is being used faster than
                                                 it can be replenished

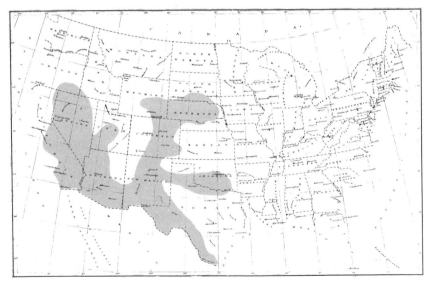

Figure 3.   Inadequate streamflow:
Inadequate Surface-Water Supply   Area where 70% of surface-water
                                                 is depleted in an average year

Some patterns of land ownership differentiate the Mountain West from the rest of the country. Farm and ranch land is more concentrated in large holdings in this region, as is shown in Table 6.

Two-thirds of the farm and ranch land in the region is owned by 5 percent of the landowners, as compared with only about one-half for the national average. Family and nonfamily corporations constitute 22.3 percent of the operating units, as compared with 8.5 percent in the nation as a whole. What these factors mean for the future of agriculture in the region is a question I leave to others.

Economically agriculture in the Mountain Region is at a slight disadvantage when compared with the national average, and the disparity appears to be growing slowly worse.[5] Since 1967, input costs (measured in constant dollars) have risen 4 percent in the Mountain Region, and 3 percent nationally. On the same index farm production is up 13 percent in this region and 21 percent nationally. Thus, input costs have been rising slightly faster and productivity has risen slightly slower than the national averages over the past ten years.

At the national level, these trends have been studied by the General Accounting Office, which has released an excellent publication that deserves wide attention. In its opening paragraph, the GAO report says,

> The United States food system's dependence on increasingly fewer farmers, who in turn are dependent on a series of factors beyond their control, raises a basic question of farm sector resiliency to withstand supply-demand fluctuations without increasing Government assistance.[6]

Of the factors that the GAO found troubling in the nation as a whole, each affects the Mountain West as much as or more than it affects the rest of the country.

One final factor affecting agriculture's future is soil erosion. The loss of topsoil through wind and water erosion is, of course, a natural process. Geologic erosion constantly wears down the land, and that is particularly true of the "young" geologic formations found in much of the West. But man's activities greatly accelerate this process, especially when the land is cultivated.

The amount of soil erosion occurring in the Mountain Region is seriously underestimated in the 1977 National Resource Inventories

Table 6. Land-Ownership Characteristics, 1978 (expressed in percentages)

Characteristic	Mountain Region	Nation
Farm & Ranch Land Owned by:		
Sole Proprietor	26.8	36.6
Husband/Wife	31.8	37.3
Family Corporations	16.7	6.1
Nonfamily Corporations	5.6	2.4
Largest 1 Percent of Owners	34	29
Largest 5 Percent of Owners	66	51
All Land, Owned by:		
Residents of Same County	77	80
Residents of Other County, Same State	13	14.5
Out-of-State Residents	10	15.5

Source. United States Department of Agriculture, Economics, Statistics, and Cooperatives Service, *Who Owns the Land?* (Washington, D.C., 1979), p. 70.

(NRI). There are several reasons for this inadequacy, most important being the lack of adequate erosion-forecasting technology adapted to the region. In estimating the 1977 erosion rates, SCS used the Universal Soil Loss Equation (USLE) to predict the erosion that would occur under field conditions that SCS technicians observed in taking the survey samples. The USLE can predict soil losses caused by sheet and rill erosion following rainfall. But in the Mountain West much of the soil erosion is caused, not by rainfall, but by melting snow or irrigation-water runoff. The USLE is not adapted for these types of erosion.

Consequently the USLE-generated estimates were very low. Only 1.4 million acres of cropland (growing three major crops) were calculated to have soil losses in excess of 5 tons per acre. Even adding land where wind erosion is a serious problem, as shown in Table 7, gives only about 615 million acres where the NRI identifies an erosion problem. In the same survey SCS technicians were asked to identify the number of acres needing conservation treatment. In those estimates, made from inspection of conditions on the land, almost 24 million acres were found to be inadequately treated. This estimate, almost four times as large as the calculated erosion rates would give us, is probably more reliable.

The major factors affecting soil erosion are the quality of the land being farmed and the amount of conservation management

Table 7. Soil-Erosion Estimates Available from the 1977 National Resource Inventories, Mountain Region (in thousands of acres)

State	Sheet and Rill Erosion (a)	Wind Erosion (b)	Total
Arizona	1		1
Colorado	624	2,420	3,044
Idaho	266		266
Montana	293	1,426	1,719
Nevada	0	0	0
New Mexico	92	1,013	1,105
Utah	1	0	1
Wyoming	102	355	457
Regional Total	1,379	5,214	6,593

(a) Acres where sheet and rill erosion was calculated to exceed 5 tons/acre/year on cropland growing corn, wheat, and sorghum.
(b) Acreage where wind erosion is a problem (Great Plains states only).
Source. USDA, SCS, "1977 National Resource Inventories."

and treatment being applied by farmers. The quality of the land cropped in the Mountain Region is significantly lower than for the nation as a whole and does not seem to be improving as rapidly as the rest of the nation. These trends are shown in Table 8.

In percentage terms, farmers in this region farm twice as much Class IV land, which is marginal for agriculture and should be cropped only in connection with an intensive conservation system. They also farm more than twice as much land in Classes V through VIII, which is classified as unsuited for cropland.

Table 8 also shows a leveling off of the region's historic shift toward farming better lands—this despite a steady rise in irrigation, which tends (at least when desert or range land is irrigated) to shift land into a higher capability class.

Almost 20 million nonfederal acres of Classes I–III land in the region are not now being cropped. But most of this land is unavailable for cropping. It is either in small ownerships or in small areas surrounded by nonagricultural lands. It may be tied up by urban development or held by its owners for that use. Whatever the cause, it is not being farmed and there is no evidence that most of it will be in the near future.

Also holding down the quality of the farmland is the fact that land-use conversions out of agriculture occur mainly on the best lands. For the region, the total acreage of cropland in Classes I through III dropped by almost a half-million acres in the past ten years. Because it is unlikely that much of this good land went out of farming for economic reasons, that may measure the *net* shifts or loss of the best lands in the region for agriculture. These losses were most strongly felt in Arizona, Colorado, New Mexico, Utah, and Wyoming.

Table 8. Trends in Cropland Quality, 1958-77, Mountain Region (expressed in percentages)

	United States			Mountain Region		
Capability Classes	1958	1967	1977	1958	1967	1977
Classes I–III	83	84	85	65	70	70
Class IV	11	11	11	23	20	21
Classes V–VIII	6	5	4	12	10	9

Sources. United States Department of Agriculture, *Basic Statistics of the National Inventory of Soil and Water Conservation Needs*, Statistical Bulletin 317 (Washington, D.C., 1962). USDA, *Inventory of Soil and Water Conservation Needs*. USDA, SCS, "1977 National Resource Inventories."

Table 9. Conservation Treatment Needs in 1977, by State. Mountain Region (in thousands of acres)

	Irrigated Cropland		Nonirrigated Cropland		Pasture & Range	
State	Treatment Needed	Treatment Not Needed	Treatment Needed	Treatment Not Needed	Treatment Needed	Treatment Not Needed
Arizona	993	283	5	30	33,754	1,349
Colorado	2,204	1,283	5,522	2,079	18,914	6,489
Idaho	1,687	1,930	1,528	1,136	5,582	2,118
Montana	1,156	1,106	5,640	7,456	28,533	12,951
Nevada	538	574	0	0	6,884	764
New Mexico	1,220	220	747	88	34,247	8,234
Utah	836	414	255	310	9,490	499
Wyoming	874	778	639	676	20,678	6,226
Regional Totals	9,508	6,588	14,336	11,775	158,082	38,630
Regional percent	59	41	55	45	80	20
National Totals	31,875	25,772	209,180	146,340	403,890	137,516
National Percentage	55	45	59	41	75	25

Source. United States Department of Agriculture, "Soil and Water Resources Conservation Act: Appraisal 1980," Review Draft, Part 1 (Washington, D.C., 1979).

Idaho, Montana, and Nevada, on the other hand, showed net gains of high-class land in agriculture over the period. These same three states also showed strong increases in irrigation in the last decade and were the only states in the region to record a net gain in the total amount of cropland during the period. The trends seem consistent.

For the region as a whole, however, the quality of cropland is low. Nor is it improving the way one would hope. In a recent survey conducted by the National Association of Conservation Districts, 49 percent of districts in this region called agricultural land conversion a serious or very serious problem in their locality.[7] One look at these data confirms their concerns. The region ought to be concerned about the conversion of high-quality agricultural land to other uses. It has none to waste.

Since a much higher erosion hazard on cropland faces this region than is true of the nation as a whole, intensive soil-conservation measures are essential. But less than half of those conservation systems are in place. About 56 percent of the cropland in the region still needs conservation treatment, as compared with 58 percent in the nation. Tables 9 and 10 indicate the treatment needs in acres as well as the percentage of cropland still needing treatment in the different capability-class groups. As is evident, the treatment levels on the irrigated cropland are about the same across all capabilities. On the drylands the Mountain Region is significantly better than the national average in Classes I through III, but the treatment of the more erosive lands lags behind.

One way to estimate soil erosion is to look at Table 9, which lists by capability class the acreages in cropland that still lack conservation treatment. The amount of erosion will vary greatly between acreages in the same capability, of course, but some rough estimates are possible. Based on limited spot data in the region, I estimate that the average annual soil-erosion rates on cropland needing treatment will be as follows:

Irrigated Cropland

Classes I–III	5 tons/acre
Class IV	15 tons/acre
Classes V–VIII	30 tons/acre

Nonirrigated Cropland

Classes I–III	7 tons/acre
Class IV	20 tons/acre
Class V–VIII	50 tons/acre

Therefore, the 24 million acres shown to need conservation treatment are deteriorating rapidly, at least 8 million of those acres losing soil at the rate of 10 tons per acre per year or more. Stated another way, at least 20 percent of this region's cropland is deteriorating at a rate that will severely restrict or completely destroy its productivity within a few decades.

Of course, both federal and nonfederal lands can replace those ruined by soil erosion or lost through conversion. We have no estimate on the amount of federal land that would, if converted, make high-quality cropland. Right now the political climate is such that there will be little if any federal land brought into agriculture in the near future. But that land is available in the event that future needs demand its conversion.

Table 11 shows the potential of the nonfederal lands for conversion to new cropland. Some 4 million acres have high potential. Of that acreage, more than one-third is in Montana. Arizona, Idaho, and New Mexico also have better than a half-million acres each that could be converted fairly easily.

Again, however, the Mountain Region is at a disadvantage when compared with the national average. Of the land not now farmed, the amount that can be cropped readily is only about one-

Table 10.   Cropland Needing Conservation Treatment in 1977, Mountain Region (expressed in percentages)

State	Irrigated Cropland			Nonirrigated Cropland		
	I-III	IV	V-VIII	I-III	IV	V-VIII
Arizona	77	100	100	50°	33°	10°
Colorado	68	57	52	71	70	87
Idaho	46	48	51	54	62	68
Montana	49	57	63	38	68	66
Nevada	50	67	33	–	–	–
New Mexico	85	82	86	88	99	· 78
Utah	63	80	77	40	49	48
Wyoming	56	61	33	56	40	40
Regional Average	60	60	49	48	67	72
National Average	55	54	56	58	66	69

°Acreages of dry cropland in Arizona are so small that the likelihood of statistical error is increased.

Source.   USDA, SCS, "1977 National Resource Inventories."

half the national potential. This disadvantage is the result of several factors, among which are—

1.   a high proportion of federal land;

2.   a low proportion of high-quality farmland;

3.   dependence on irrigation water supplies not always adequate for current demands and not always available where irrigable land exists;

4.   growing competition for limited land and water supplies from nonagricultural consumers;

5.   agricultural input costs, which are rising slightly faster than the national average; and farm productivity, which is rising slightly slower;

6.   a steady and continuous loss of agricultural productivity to both soil erosion and farmland conversion;

7.   a limited potential for adding new high-quality cropland to replace the land being lost;

8.   rising energy costs that will discriminate most heavily against intensively irrigated agriculture—particularly where that water must

Table 11.   Potential for Cropland of 1977 Pasture, Range, Forest, and Other Lands by State, Mountain Region (in thousands of acres)

State	High Potential	Medium Potential	Conversion Unlikely	Zero Potential	Totals
Arizona	589	402	5,500	31,831	38,322
Colorado	377	2,438	8,588	18,738	30,141
Idaho	583	971	1,942	8,985	12,481
Montana	1,428	4,326	11,710	31,770	49,234
Nevada	58	451	2,635	6,026	9,170
New Mexico	537	860	13,379	33,141	47,917
Utah	82	523	1,544	11,847	13,996
Wyoming	297	1,778	7,013	19,949	29,037
Regional Totals	3,951	11,749	52,311	162,289	230,398
Regional Percentage	2	5	23	70	100
National Totals	40,082	94,917	299,257	548,487	982,643
National Percentage	4	10	30	56	100
Regional Total as Percentage of National	10	12			

Source.   USDA, SCS, "1977 National Resource Inventories."

be pumped from deep wells or river canyons; and

9.   a disadvantageous freight-rate structure aggravated by big distances and low concentrations of agricultural product, by limited regional population and food demand, and by the increasing proportion of American farm products that must be moved to export ports.

Nothing in the current data or trends indicates that the region's agricultural disadvantages will end in the near future. Some indicators—such as the forecast growth in energy production and its associated water demands—suggest increasing difficulty for the region's agricultural industry. The situation calls for immediate attention to remedies. The time to move against worrisome trends in land use and management is *before* the situation "goes critical."

In closing I would like to quote Congressman Jim Jeffords of Vermont. His views, aimed at the national situation, are particularly appropriate for this region.

> We have time to act in a reasonable manner. We have 24 million acres of reserve farmland. They are disappearing fast, but we can still begin to protect the remaining farmland in a way that will not infringe upon legitimate individual rights. We have a six-inch average layer of topsoil. That's not much, but we have time to begin rebuilding it without regimenting our farmers into a maze of bureaucratic regulations from Washington.
>
> We have time to act reasonably and fairly, without imposing undue controls over people's lives. But we don't have time to waste. The longer we wait, the more drastic the action that will be required to avert unthinkable human suffering in this country. If we begin now, it's not a minute too soon.[8]

An Eye for Horses and Men

Well, Billy Brown and me went to look
    at a blue horse over at a neighbor's ranch.
Rode him around the arena a couple of times
    and asked the price...

"If I had the money, I'd buy him," Billy advised.
       "I wouldn't quibble
about two or three hundred dollars."
So I bought that horse for a pretty high price,
      and took him home to Guadalupe.
    Billy rode him for three months.

"This horse ought to be worth all the other horses
    you've got on this ranch," Billy said.
But he was a head-throwin',
      star-gazin' son of a gun three months later
    when Billy got done ridin' him up and down the canyon.

So I rode him pretty hard and regular for another 10 months or so,
    and showed him to Bill Bryan one day in the spring.
Spun him around in little circles, figure eighted him
    and had him near lopin' backwards, but really...
      couldn't seem to get him to do things right.

'I don't know what it is about him,' I say to Bill,
   'I keep workin' with him, hopin' maybe
         someday he'll come around.
He'd sure make a top rope horse, or a barrel,
      or a pole horse for the kids.
   What do you think? Have you ever seen a horse
   with that much action before?'

"The penitentiary is full of guys with good action,"
   Bill Bryan says. "Better look there into his eyes,
   that's where you'll see what counts."

                                             Drum Hadley

Part Two
Human Resources

Leonard J. Arrington is Lemuel Redd Professor of Western History in Brigham Young University and Historian of the Church of Jesus Christ of Latter-day Saints. He is the author of several books, including *Great Basin Kingdom: An Economic History of the Latter-day Saints, 1830-1900*, and *The Mormon Experience*, recently published with Davis Bitton.

Isao Fujimoto is an author and educator at the University of California, Davis. His publications include works on strengthening the family farm in the United States.

R. Keith Higginson is Commissioner, Water and Power Resources Service (formerly the Bureau of Reclamation) in the Department of the Interior.

William K. Everson has authored twelve books on film including *The Western: From Silents to the Seventies* (with George N. Fenin) and *A Pictorial History of the Western*. He has written extensively for *Western Film Annual, Films and Filming, Sight and Sound, Cinema, Cinema Nuovo, Films in Review, Film, Culture, Film Comment, The New York Times*, and *The New York Times Book Review*. He is currently on the faculties in the School of Visual Arts, the New School of Social Research, and New York University.

Can the Family Farm Survive?

Leonard J. Arrington

A survey of 1,700 Idaho households showed that 94 percent think the family farm is important to the state's overall culture. I don't think you could get percentages that high for motherhood and apple pie. And I doubt that such a high proportion could sing "And Here We Have Idaho." It also showed that 67 percent would be willing to pay 5 percent more for food to insure the survival of the family farm.[1]

Despite the almost universal agreement on goals, it won't hurt us to remind ourselves of the human values perpetuated by the family farm and to consider ways we can preserve and strengthen it.

Surely the family farm can be strengthened by strengthening the family, but I assume we are not going to concern ourselves with the sociology—with the ways to strengthen the family itself.

First, some statistics:

1. The size of the typical family farm of early Rocky Mountain settlements was 20 acres, as compared with today's 160 acres. We are talking here of irrigated farms, not ranches that graze sheep or cattle.

2. The number of persons living on farms is increasing. Although the total farm population is declining, the number of people living on the farms that produce the bulk of the nation's food and fiber is increasing. For example, in the 1970s the farm population declined about 13 percent, but the number of persons living on farms with significant sales increased 76 percent. The total 1970-75 farm population decline occurred among farm residents without regard to

[65]

race, operator status, or region of residence. Losses were heavier in the nonoperator population than the operator population; the population of blacks declined faster than whites; and the population living on southern farms dropped at a greater rate than in the northern and western states.

3.   Of the total farm population, about 60 percent reside on farms operated by a full owner. About 30 percent are on part-owner-operated farms, and about 10 percent are on tenant or managed farms.

4.   Of the total United States farm population, about two-thirds live on livestock and grain farms. Forty percent of all farm people live on livestock farms, 30 percent on cash-grain farms.

5.   If needed, 100 million acres could yet be placed in production.[2]

We may affirm three basic propositions. The first is that the agricultural policy of the United States has always been based upon a commitment to traditional agrarian values. Much of our legislation has been predicated on the belief that the family farm was, in a special sense, a source of civic virtue—not a unique source of virtue, but an important source nevertheless. Settlers on the land have been regarded as persons of honesty, industry, and morality—the backbone of our democracy, and the mainstay of our economy. To those interested in furthering free enterprise, the family farm unquestionably promotes it.

There may be a few who argue that the family farm is outmoded and inefficient, but most agricultural economists believe it is an efficient producer of food, a conserver of soil and water resources, a bulwark of community stability, an antidote to pollution, and a good way of life. It promotes both freedom and security.

History also suggests that rearing children on farms promotes the work ethic: Farm children learn how to work.

Family farms also promote individuality. Rural culture permits idiosyncratic personality development. Much of our richest folklore relates to rural personalities, whether in Russia, Italy, Ireland, France, England, or the United States.

The second basic proposition is that the world population is increasing alarmingly, which means an increasing demand for food. The most efficient and productive suppliers of food are the irrigated farms and ranches of the West. And the most numerous and most efficient of these are the family farms. Therefore, it is in the interest

of the nation and the world that the family farm be protected and encouraged.

As Ellis Armstrong, former Commissioner of Reclamation and a noted consultant on water, has pointed out, the world population is now about 4.3 billion. It is expected to increase to 8 or 9 billion by the year 2020—forty years from now. The industrialized countries of western Europe, North America, Japan, Australia, and New Zealand now constitute 18 percent of world population. This will decrease to 11 percent by 2020. The centrally planned countries, USSR and China and their satellites, have 30 percent of world population. That will decrease to about 24 percent by 2020. The developing countries, with about 52 percent of the world's population, will increase to about 65 percent by 2020.[3]

In a short statement in the 15 September 1979 issue of *Saturday Review*, Robert Rice stated,

> The one commodity this nation produces that stands head and shoulders above the rest of the world [is] food. Without agricultural exports as the one bright spot in our balance-of-payments picture, our economy wouldn't just be in trouble, it would collapse.... [Indeed] we have such a reliable affordable food supply that we take for granted the one product that sustains life. Only someone with a full stomach can afford the

luxury of worrying about who makes the best cameras and racing cars.

The increased population will require irrigation acreage in the United States and elsewhere. There must be a more effective and efficient use of the world's agricultural resources. And that is true of the West's resources as well. Much of the nation's future supply of energy is in the West.

The Mountain States contain 45 percent of the nation's coal reserves, and enough oil shale to last the nation two hundred years. We must be prepared to supply food to the ever greater numbers of people who will be extracting these resources.

To preserve and nurture the family farm and at the same time supply ever-increasing amounts of food, we must have (1) the best possible management of our water resources, (2) the best possible management of our land resources, and (3) the best possible management of our human resources.

The single most important problem of agriculture in the West, and one that is crucial to the family farm, is the provision of adequate water for irrigation. We must determine to utilize the West's scarce water resources to their maximum in irrigated agriculture. Many western farms, of course, rely upon artesian flow rather than upon rivers, dams, and canals. High-speed pumps of marvelous efficiency draw up hundreds of gallons per minute from depths as great as 1,500 feet. Much is invested in these deep borings. With such heavy investment, crops must bring good and steady prices to avert catastrophe. No other farmers in America risk such fortunes against market trends as do our irrigators in the West.

Of like concern is the mishandling of water. Many poorly managed irrigation districts lose half their water between the reservoir and the farms serviced. Engineers estimate that between 20 and 50 percent more land could be irrigated, without adding another dam or well, if only water now available were delivered to fields in paved canals.

Another concern is the conservation of the soil itself. Every year we are losing the equivalent of an inch or two of topsoil from the two million acres on the federal range alone. The destination of this eroded earth, so essential to the rancher, is the water reservoir of the irrigator, who certainly doesn't want it there. We must protect our land from further deterioration.

My third basic proposition is that it is in the interest of the nation to assist in the development of *western agriculture.* For one thing, the productivity of western agriculture is far higher than that in the remainder of the nation. That is, the net return of agricultural labor and management is higher in the West than for the nation. The higher productivity of our irrigated cropland is derived from the higher degree of control that the farmer can exercise in its use. The farmer can supply water at the time and in the amounts needed and can usually count on higher yields per acre. Consequently, he is willing to risk a heavy investment in the intensive cultivation of the land—a factor that again requires stable and remunerative prices.

This control, and the general climatic and soil conditions, make our irrigated land particularly well adapted to the production of vegetables and fruit—precisely the products in great demand in our high-income economy. Moreover, western irrigated cropland and pastures provide supplementary feed for range livestock and make possible a high degree of efficiency in the production of meat animals.

Farmers are subject to costs they no longer control. In the days of horse farming, the farmer's costs were generated within the farm economy. Feeds and fertilizer were produced on the farm. Insecticides and pesticides were fewer and less expensive. Power was provided by men and animals. Farmers had considerable control over these inputs and their attendant costs. Today farmers are dependent on steelworkers, truckers, dockworkers. They depend on government policy, which has often denied them traditional weapons against insects, rodents, and plant diseases. They depend on the Organization of Petroleum Exporting Countries (OPEC). This has created economic instability, focusing increased attention on the policies of our government and the governments of other countries. Because they must invest heavily, farmers depend on government to help stabilize prices and incomes. They require government action, not to meddle, but to maintain stability.

The fivefold increase in the price of petroleum during the 1970s, for example, has slowed the growth of energy use in agriculture—not only in tractors and irrigation pumps, but also, indirectly, in the supply and price of chemical fertilizers.

Finally, the family farm is threatened by what one critic has called land cannibalism. Cities have insatiable appetites for land.

In 1941, for example, the county of Los Angeles had 2.7 million
people and 300,000 acres of tilled land—a ratio of 9 to 1. By 1975
the ratio had shot up to 133 to 1. In the United States as a whole,
the U.S. Department of Agriculture reports, more than 6 million
acres of prime cropland were converted to urban and build-up uses
between 1967 and 1976.

In Utah 20 percent of the land is in farms. The amount increased steadily until 1950, when 1.3 million acres were in cropland. Because of urban development, cropland in Salt Lake County
dropped from 93,000 acres in 1959 to 57,000 acres in 1974. At the
present rate no more cropland will exist in Salt Lake County by
the year 2003.[4]

The most successful preservation accomplished at the county
and municipal level includes the following: innovative zoning (with
quarter-quarter system and/or performance zones), assessment
benefits, purchase or compensation for some development rights,
decreased taxes for farmland, and adjusted inheritance taxes (free-
ing inheritors from the need to sell land to developers to pay taxes).

We need a new land ethic, a new reverence for the land—a
better understanding of our dependence on a vital resource that we
cannot afford to take for granted.

As William Everson said about the movie of French farm life, *Farrebique,* viewing a family farm as a purely *economic* enterprise is a mistake. There can be joy in farming, and many remain on farms because they enjoy the way of life.

During the Great Depression of the late 1920s in England and continental Europe and in the 1930s in the United States, there arose a whole literature about the advantages of the wide distribution of property and the wide participation of people in farming activities. This included the English Distributionists: Gilbert Keith Chesterton, Douglas Jerrold, and Hilaire Belloc; such Spanish writers as Ortega y Gasset and Salvador de Madariaga; Norwegian writers like Knut Hamsun; and many Russian writers, especially Tolstoy. American writers of the depression era produced many works on this theme: Ellen Glasgow, *Vein of Iron;* Pearl Buck, *The Good Earth;* Ole Rolvaag, *Giants in the Earth.* And there are the writings of the Southern agrarians: Allan Tate, John Crowe Ransom, Herbert Agar, Robert Penn Warren, Frank Owsley, and others.

These people were not economists. They revolted too strongly against modernism, and some of their ideas came to be discredited. Nevertheless, they had a vision of a nation made up of a proud yeomanry working with God on widely distributed farms, living lives of individual and civic virtue. I leave with you that vision as worthy of remembrance.

Farming in the Rockies: A Humanistic Perspective

Isao Fujimoto

At the risk of sounding grandiose I would like to spend a few minutes discussing the human aspects of farming from a grand scale: the farmer as artist, as a reflection of policies on war and peace, as affecting the quality of life in human settlements, and as providing a philosophical view on the world. These topics are global, but they also have direct bearing on the Rockies.

One way to get an impression of the impact of farmers in the Rockies is to see the farmscape, not from the ground level, but from six miles up. If the earth is looked on as an artist's canvas, the artwork created by agriculturalists matches that of any modern artist. In fact, we have a new school of concept artists who use the earth as part of the art, stringing miles of cloth fences through the pastures of Sonoma County to the Pacific Ocean, or draping the Grand Canyon in one giant sheet. However, I think the farmer has surpassed anything the concept artist can produce. Those of you who have had window seats on a clear day flying across this country and have seen the dramatic designs created by various farming systems can attest to this.

Whether it is an oasis in North Africa, plantations in Sumatra or Hawaii, or irrigated farms in the Midwest, the result can be seen as the work of artists. But as an art, farming offers not just the beauty to contemplate, but also a message. Contrast a vegetable farm near Hong Kong with those in the Imperial Valley, the terraces of Japan with coffee groves in Brazil, the centuries-old drainage patterns of farms in Austria and Denmark with the center-pivot irrigation systems in Colorado. Farms and farmers have made an imprint on the face of the earth. Some blend in ecologically where the farm-scape is part of the landscape. Others are forerunners of scars on the earth. These have a direct bearing on the future of farms in the Rockies.

Farming is also a reflection of war and peace. The development of farming in the Rockies, for example, paralleled the technology of warfare. Every major breakthrough in farming technology used here is a by-product of war—fertilizers, mechanization, insecticides, herbicides, and so on. Let's start with fertilizers. At the time Alfred Nobel invented dynamite, the major source of nitrates (also important in the manufacture of explosives) was the guano deposits in Chile. The development of the Haber Process for the artificial fixation of nitrogen enabled the Germans (who no longer had to worry about being cut off from Chilean guano) to launch World War I. After the war the question was how to take advantage of this industrial breakthrough. An obvious application was in farming.

We also saw, after the first World War, a shift from the use of animal power to tractor power. One need only look at a documentary history of a major farm-implement company like Caterpillar Tractor to see the interchange between tractors and tanks. After each major war—World War I, World War II, the Korean War—both horsepower and sophisticated methods of production were transferred from the manufacture of tanks to that of tractors.

As for pesticides, they are truly an afterthought of a product created for warfare. In the course of chemical-warfare research, some chemicals were thought to be lethal to insects, which ironically were used as "guinea pigs" to test agents that would bring death to humans. The legacy of the Vietnam War is defoliants, which translate into herbicides. They are principal agents of a scorched-earth policy in Southeast Asia, which now suffers long-term ecological consequences. The dangerous lessons defoliants teach us are now very close to home. Community groups throughout the Northwest are increasingly protesting the spraying of their communities, which spraying supposedly will benefit the timber industry and the U.S. Forest Service.

As for farms and how they have impact on the human settlement, both everyday observations and detailed research show the relation between the skill of agriculture and the quality of life in rural communities. I can share with you some of my observations from my study of 130 towns in the eight San Joaquin Valley counties of California. For instance, I was struck by the fact that, although these are the most productive farming areas in the United States, ranking at the top economically in terms of agricultural commodities, they also have the largest percentage of families with the lowest income in the state. How could it be that the richest agricultural areas could have also the poorest people? Because information focusing only on counties tends to obliterate differences that might exist among towns, I looked at all 130 towns rather than compare eight counties. Within the same county there are well-to-do towns and poor ones—not just in terms of income, but also in services and spirit. To determine what influences communities to be what they are, I graded them on the basis of how well they utilized the two resources most important to valley agriculture—land and water.

Land can be used for large-scale or small-scale farming, and decisions on agricultural water use can be democratic or nondemocratic. For the study, "large" farms as judged by the cropping patterns shown on aerial photographs, referred to places where the predominant size was a section (640 acres) or larger. In contrast, "small" meant that the predominant pattern of land use was less than a quarter-section (160 acres). Though there are many types of jurisdictions for the management of water resources in California, these can be sorted out into two basic types—places where decisions are made on the basis of one-person/one-vote, and those where one dollar or one acre brings one vote. The former I called "democratic"; the latter, "nondemocratic."

Also, all 130 towns were analyzed in terms of the services available to the residents and were ranked accordingly—from the most complex to the least differentiated. Thus, the 130 towns could be sorted according to their complexity, whether they were in areas dominated by large- or small-scale farming, and whether or not they were in democratic or nondemocratic water jurisdictions.

I can best sum up the findings in this way. First of all, large-scale farming and lack of democracy are not conducive to community building. The areas characterized by large-scale farming and nondemocratic water jurisdictions had few communities to speak of. Second, where comparisons could be made, the towns in areas surrounded by small-scale farming and democratic water systems had more choice in services, both in terms of variety and number, than did towns of comparable size located where large-scale farms and nondemocratic water systems dominated.

But the relation between skill of farming and quality of life may be more obvious on an everyday level. As the famous Bob Dylan song out of the sixties reminds us, "You don't need a weatherman to tell you which way the wind is blowing." Enough of us who have lived in small towns, who observe the changing scenery in rural America, know that the dynamics of life in a small agricultural town are very much affected by the health of the family farm. When they are being blown away, so is the town. When family farms are viable, there is vitality in the community.

All this brings us to the last point about the relation between family farming and a philosophy of life. Last year, people associated with the FARM conference (the Northern Rockies Action Group) brought together two disparate groups—sheep ranchers and environmentalists—to discuss the future of the Rockies. The most impressive aspect of the gathering was the discovery of the commonalities between the two, rather than their differences. I think a similar situation exists among the seemingly disparate groups associated with the family-farm issue. People connected with the ecology movement, civil rights, appropriate technology, community development, local control, alternative energy—all see something vital in the perseverance of the family farm. What all these people and groups share is a world view and a set of values in marked contrast to the exploitative, dependency-creating priorities held by the dominant corporate interests, monopolies, and bureaucracies.

The values shared by people associated with the family farm, be it in the Rockies or elsewhere, include: a concern with accountability—not just economic, but ecological and social—for long-term as well as immediate needs; self-reliance and decentralized approaches to self-sufficiency rather than the dependency on centrally concentrated experts and resources; genuine competition and cooperation rather than monopolies attempting to seduce the public into believing that all this trend toward concentration will benefit the consumers in terms of efficiency and cost savings. Taken together—accountability as contrasted with exploitation, self-reliance over dependency, diversity and decentralization versus concentration of power and resources, and cooperation instead of monopoly—we are talking not only about what unites people concerned with the perseverance of the family farm, but also about a more responsible way of looking at the world.

The 160-Acre Limitation

R. Keith Higginson

It is safe to say that the bill before the United States Senate (No. S-14) will satisfy no one. The members of the Senate, after debating amendments for two full days, accepted some compromises that did not meet their expectations. The large landowners, who were fighting to retain the federal water subsidy for their multi-thousand-acre operations, are upset that an acreage limit would be imposed on them. The small farmers are unwilling to accept the large farm size permitted or the lack of a residency requirement. The Administration is disappointed that the bill would stray so far away from the basic intent of reclamation law. And I personally— the individual charged with administering the law—am concerned with the numerous inconsistencies and technical problems that would make it impossible to administer. The bill is in need of improvement.[1]

But before we address the bill itself, let us review some history.

Following the United States' acquisition of the territories that now constitute the public-land states of the West, Congress passed several laws related to public occupation, settlement, and cultivation of those lands. These included the Homestead Act, the Desert Land Act, and the Carey Act. Each had as its purpose the encouragement of private acquisition of public land to promote the settlement and taming of the West. With the Carey Act of 1894, Congress recognized the need for group effort in the financing and construction of water-supply works in the arid parts of the West, where irrigation is essential for agriculture. Group efforts under state supervision had been largely unsuccessful except here in Idaho, where companies were formed and about 600,000 acres of desert land were reclaimed and land patents issued.

With the 1900s came an awareness that the successful colonization of the West was dependent on direct federal assistance. The 1902 Reclamation Act was the answer. It provided that the proceeds from the sale of public lands would be placed in a fund that could be used to finance the construction of dams, reservoirs, and canals to provide a water supply. The Secretary of the Interior was charged with this responsibility, and he responded by creating the Reclamation Service within the U.S. Geological Survey.

In all these public-land laws, Congress included acreage and other limitations to assure that the benefits of the relatively free land and subsidized water supply did not accumulate in the hands of a few.

The Reclamation Act had four purposes:

1. to settle the West through the federally subsidized development of water resources for irrigated agriculture,

2. to foster an agriculture based on the family farm (as is manifest in limitations on farm size and personal operatorship),

3. to distribute widely the benefits of federal public works, and

4. to assure that the subsidy that goes with the land is not allowed to accumulate in the hands or pockets of a few or to benefit land speculators rather than legitimate farmers.

Of course the settlement of the West has long since been achieved, but the other purposes have continuing validity.

To appreciate fully the current debate on this issue requires an understanding of the nature of the subsidy.

The irrigation subsidy originally authorized by the Reclamation Act of 1902 was, in retrospect, very limited. The act required that *all* project costs be repaid to the Treasury by the irrigator-beneficiaries within ten years. The only subsidy was the forgiveness of interest for the decade. In 1906 Congress authorized the Secretary to sell surplus power from reclamation projects and credit the revenues to the reclamation fund. Because production of power for resale was not a major purpose of early reclamation projects, this feature did not substantially reduce irrigators' repayment obligations, and the irrigation subsidy remained very limited.

In 1914 Congress extended the repayment period to twenty years, and in 1926 to forty years. Irrigators still repaid substantially all costs of the project, so the principal subsidy remained in the forgiveness of interest on the debt. Because interest rates were low in the first half of this century, averaging less than 3 percent, the interest-free aspect continued to have limited impact on the Treasury.

The 1939 Reclamation Project Act was enacted during a period of severe agricultural depression, when reclamation agriculture, like that elsewhere, was hard hit. The act led to major changes in reclamation repayment. First, it expressly allowed a "development period" of up to ten years, which effectively extended the irrigators' repayment period to fifty years. The other important change it made was the way it authorized other beneficiaries of the project to pay part of the irrigators' costs. Specifically, irrigators are to be charged only an "appropriate share" of the project costs (that portion of the costs of the project allocated to irrigation and within the irrigator's ability to pay"). Any part of the costs of an irrigation project that is above an irrigator's ability to pay is to be paid by purchasers of project-generated municipal or industrial water or power. Thus, irrigators do not repay all project costs "allocated to irrigation"; rather, power consumers and other customers pay a large share.

The costs allocated to irrigation and repaid by power consumers and other customers are also paid without interest. In short, irrigators themselves pay, without interest, only the portion of the cost that is within their "ability to pay"—what they are judged able to afford. The rest is subsidized by the Treasury (forgiveness of interest on the entire cost allocated to the irrigation function) and by power and other consumers.

The shift from a limited subsidy in 1902 to a heavy subsidy in 1939 occurred without any congressional statement regarding increased public assistance for reclamation irrigation. As a result, because the "excess lands" restrictions remained on the books, the original reclamation objectives became the justification for the growing subsidy, continuing to ensure that it would not be concentrated in the hands of a comparatively few speculators or investors. An additional result is the fact that relatively few major reclamation-irrigation investments were made until several years after the 1939 Act, so that the full impact of the 1939 Act is only now beginning to be realized. No comprehensive analysis of the subsidy has been done, but the available information on specific

projects facilitates realistic subsidy calculations. For example, the fact that Imperial Valley irrigators repay the cost of their water storage and delivery system without interest over a half-century means the Treasury will forego interest of between $260 million (assuming an interest rate of 3 percent) and $770 million (assuming an interest rate of 5 percent). There are 440,000 acres in the Imperial Valley. Thus, the interest subsidy alone is worth $591 to $1,750 per acre. The figures for some newer projects show even more impressive subsidies over a presumed fifty-year repayment period. Using the interest rate of 6 percent, the interest forgiveness will cost taxpayers nearly $1.6 billion in the Auburn-Folsom South Unit of the Central Valley Project, slightly more than that in the Central Arizona Project, and nearly $4.4 billion in the Columbia Basin Project.

No one argues that such subsidies are unjustified—everything the federal government does is subsidizing some segment of society. But unless there are some reasonable controls, these subsidies will accumulate in the pockets of a few at the expense of all.

With this background, let us review the provisions of S.14 and the position of the Department of Reclamation with respect to this bill.

Applicability. Federal Reclamation law shall apply only to lands in an authorized Federal Reclamation project pursuant to a contract with the United States.

The Department supports tightening of this provision to assure that lands receiving irrigation water from Bureau of Reclamation and Corps of Engineer projects are covered.

Acreage Entitlement. S. 14 limits irrigation water deliveries to 1,280 acres of land owned and/or leased by a qualified recipient.

The Senate rejected two amendments that would have reduced the entitlement to 640 acres and 960 acres respectively. Also rejected was an amendment to permit water deliveries to lands held in excess of 1,280 acres upon payment of a graduated surcharge on the excess lands.

The Department favors a 960-acre family-unit entitlement owned and/or leased.

Leasing Restrictions. Land leased over and above the 1,280-acre entitlement would not be eligible for irrigation-water service. The provision in S.14, as reported by the Senate Committee, for unrestricted leasing on an annual basis was deleted by action of the Senate. Also rejected were two amendments that would have permitted water deliveries to land leased in excess of 1,280 acres upon payment of interest on the unpaid balance of the project costs allocated to irrigation. Under S.14 as approved, leased land must be included in the 1,280-acre entitlement.

The Department proposes that a 960-acre entitlement, including leased land, be provided.

Equivalency. The use of Class I equivalency to determine the acreage entitlement based on 1,280 acres of Class I land would be authorized for all projects under S.14. The use of Class I equivalency will increase the acreage entitlement in most cases.

The Department supports the use of Class I equivalency on a project-by-project basis in areas with a frost-free growing season of 180 days or fewer.

Exemptions. Land held by religious and charitable nonprofit organizations as of 1 January 1978 and used for charitable purposes would be exempt.

The Department favors this exemption.

Lands within the Imperial Irrigation District in California as of 1 January 1979 would be exempt, except that lands acquired in excess of 1,280 acres subsequently can be served upon payment of interest on the remaining obligation allocated to such land.

The Department favors deletion of the Imperial exemption and application of the acreage-limitation provisions to the Imperial District.

Landholdings benefited by Corps of Engineers projects are exempt under S.14 as approved unless (1) the project is integrated with a federal reclamation project, (2) project works have been provided under reclamation law for the control or conveyance of agricultural water, or (3) federal reclamation laws are made applicable by statute. An amendment that was approved would make the acreage-limitation provisions applicable to the Kings, Kern, Kaweah, and Tule River projects in California with the provision that the Kings and Kern River projects would be relieved from acreage limitation upon payment of the costs attributable to providing storage for such purposes.

The Department favors application of acreage limitation to the lands served by the four Corps projects in California.

Residency. The residency requirement of reclamation law would be repealed by S.14 as approved.

The Department supports a requirement that the recipient of federal project water live within fifty miles of the land and be substantially involved in the farming operation.

Repayment of Construction Charges. Acreage limitation shall cease to apply to a contracting entity that has its construction obligation in accordance with the terms of its contract with the United States. Lump-sum or accelerated payments would not be permitted as a result of amendment approved by the Senate.

The Department does not favor payout alone as a basis for exemption unless the Secretary of the Interior determines that a general pattern of family-size farms has been established except for certain contracts containing payout provisions that have been executed but that Congress has not validated.

Disposition of Excess Lands. The owner of excess land will be permitted to dispose of that land to a purchaser of his choice during the term of a recordable contract (specified to be ten years). If the excess land is not sold within that term, a power of attorney will vest with the Secretary of the Interior, who will select the buyer by lottery. Rejected was an amendment to require that the owner of excess land sell that land by lottery during the recordable contract disposition period.

The Department favors provision for a recordable contract with a five-year disposition period beginning when federal project water is available to the land.

Other Provisions. Several other amendments to reclamation law and its administrative provisions are incorporated in S.14 as approved. Of particular interest is a provision that permits contracting entities to bring an action in the U.S. District Court against the United States to incorporate written representations that may have been made in its contract.

The Department opposes this consent-to-sue provision.

We are very hopeful that the House will now take the Senate bill and make improvements on it that would bring it in line with the original purposes of the Reclamation Act but that also would take into account the substantial changes in farm practices and economics since 1902. In the absence of such improvements in the law, the Department of Reclamation will have no choice but to enforce the present 160-acre limit and residency provisions.

Hollywood and Agriculture: A Survey

William K. Everson

Three of America's biggest industries are (and have been, for many years) steel, newspapers, and agriculture. Hollywood has done quite well by the steel industry, even if it has seen it in the somewhat repetitive terms of vehicles for flint-and-steel personalities like Milton Sills, Randolph Scott, and John Wayne. The newspaper industry has been handled as melodrama, as satire, and as a vehicle for protest. That particular cycle, which peaked in the early thirties, was revived in recent years, reaching its apparent climax with *All the President's Men*. Because movie newspapermen were always after that "big story," there was just no topping the biggest story of them all—the toppling of a government. Consequently, since then Hollywood seems to have unofficially exiled—or retired—the newspaper movie.

But Hollywood has never admitted the dramatic (and only rarely the documentary) values of agriculture. Boiled down to box-office and profit considerations, the rationale seems to be that the big metropolitan audiences have no interest in agricultural themes and that the farm belts (which, after all, form a pretty hefty chunk of the nation's box offices) are too close to the problems of drought and weather and poverty to find dramatic or other entertainment value in them. Even before television changed the nation's moviegoing habits, Hollywood had long characterized "folksy" films as being what agricultural audiences would buy: films like *The Country Doctor, I'd Climb the Highest Mountain*, the hillbilly musical comedies of the Weaver Brothers and Judy Canova, and the Will

[83]

Rogers vehicles of the early thirties. Undoubtedly there is more drama in the farmer's perpetual fight against weather and economics than in the day-to-day life of a country preacher. But the latter lent itself to personalized and often highly sentimentalized treatments. As a result, the preacher became a kind of folk-hero, but the farmer never did—and probably never will. (At the end of the twenties, inspired by Byrd and Lindbergh, the aviator/explorer took over from the cowboy as the movies' national hero—only to be replaced during the depression years by the idealistic and self-sacrificing doctor (a figure who could operate realistically in *all* the social milieus of the thirties).

With some rare exceptions (of which more in a moment), Hollywood saw the farmer in two terms: as a background for comedy, and as a background for melodrama and action. Mack Sennett's *Down on the Farm* typified, in the silent period, the farmyard as a convenient backdrop for mayhem: malfunctioning water pumps and wells and aggressive goats. Chaplin and most of the other great silent comedians served their apprenticeship in "farm" comedies, and the tradition was carried on into sound comedies by everybody from Abbott and Costello to the Jones Family (who also made a *Down on the Farm*) and the Hardy Family, reaching a zenith (or nadir) with the Ma and Pa Kettle series of the forties and fifties.

In terms of melodrama, the farmer became a useful victim. If Hollywood was unconcerned with the long-range drama in growing and nurturing products—livestock, fruit, or vegetable—it saw immediate plot material in the racketeering involved in merchandising those products. Big-city truckers were the invariable villains, putting the small farmers out of business via their high transportation rates or low purchase prices in the big-city markets. In *St. Louis Kid* James Cagney broke up a milk-price war; in *Racket Busters* Humphrey Bogart had a stranglehold on market prices; and in *Thieves' Highway* labor racketeer Lee J. Cobb was paying rock-bottom prices for apples. "B" westerns came up with quite a few novelties: In *Headin' East* Buck Jones was fighting for a better deal for lettuce growers, and in *Hawaiian Buckaroo* the villains were out to take over a pineapple plantation!

Westerns, "A" and "B", not infrequently tackled ecology problems. Roy Rogers' *Under Western Stars* dealt rather seriously with the problems of the Dust Bowl states long before *The Grapes of Wrath* got around to it, and Gene Autry's *Sierra Sue* was unique in that the only villain was poison weed, and the only real conflict was the farmers' battle with that weed. (Villains or none, the script contrived to work in the required amount of riding, fighting, shooting Autry action, although it was ingeniously and even intelligently introduced.) Further south, the problems of sharecroppers raising cotton—in films like Warners' early thirties *Cabin in the Cotton* —were again social rather than essentially agricultural: Exploitation by the landowners, a lynching, and some sexual fireworks between Bette Davis and Richart Barthelmess dominated the narrative.

Perhaps because wheat itself has a symbolic quality, and because wheat farming can be pictorially lyrical (and simple land inexpensive to shoot), Hollywood has done rather better by that branch of agriculture. To shoot *City Girl* (a silent made in 1929 under the title of *Our Daily Bread*) German director F. W. Murnau rented an entire wheat farm in Oregon and shot most of the film there. It was the kind of film that attracted many prestige directors in the late silent period: a contrast between an outsider and country people, and the conflict between city and country life, frequently expressed via battles against the elements. Such films as *The Canadian, White Gold,* and *The Wind* were in this mold. *City Girl* was one of the best. Although it was a story about people, its story was so slight that the story of wheat came very much to the fore.

Ten years later, John Steinbeck's *Of Mice and Men* was even more a story about people, but its California wheatfield backgrounds provided some memorable images (especially in the original prints, released in rich sepia tones) plus, if accidentally, some almost documentary insights into that phase of agriculture. But more common— and far more commercial—were films like *Wild Harvest,* in which gangs of wheat harvesters fought each other en masse, while Alan Ladd battled individually with Robert Preston over Dorothy Lamour! One of the most interesting wheat westerns was *Gold Is Where You Find It,* which substituted a wheat-farmer/gold-miner conflict for the traditional sheepman/cattleman range war. In the newly perfected three-color Technicolor system, agriculture—golden gain and fruit orchards (plus the rosy cheeks of Olivia de Haviland)— won hands down, pictorially as well as ecologically, over mining. Just the color of the muddy, polluted rivers could turn the miners into the heavies.

There are, of course, exceptions to these generalizations. D. W. Griffith's silent *Way Down East* and Henry King's sound remake both added a sense of the importance and beauty of the land, and the dignity of farming as a profession, to the old-hat melodrama of the original play. *Come Next Spring*, an unjustly ignored film of the fifties, used the resilience and the "eternal" quality of farmland (specifically Arkansas) as a backdrop to the dramatic story of a man's reformation. King Vidor's *Our Daily Bread* of 1934 was an overly optimistic but sincerely felt hymn to the land—and to farming—as America's prime salvation during the depression years. *Our Vines Have Tender Grapes* was a nonclichéd, offbeat slice of life from California's grape-growing areas. And more than once in themes of Americana, farming has been equated with all that is good in America. For example, in *The Devil and Daniel Webster*, Stephen Vincent Benet's New England fantasy, the farmer sells his soul to the Devil but is saved by the eloquence of Daniel Webster, whose pleas to a ghostly jury include near-rhapsodic tributes to the richness and fertility of the soil.

Hollywood has never seen the farmer as a potential hero. On the other hand, in such propagandistic set-pieces as Eisenstein's *The Old and the New*, the Soviet Union made the farmer and his tractor almost the equivalent of the American cowboy. British love of land and open country accounted for several farmer heroes in their movies. But Hollywood somehow typed the American farmer as good, honest, much-put-upon by the elements and his creditors, but essentially rather stolid, stubborn, and unwilling to change with the times. Invariably his problems were solved by outsiders from the city. It may well have been Hollywood's inability to see the farmer as hero that has caused agriculture in general to be used only as a background in American films.

It is significant surely that the few—and the best—American films on farming have been notably non-Hollywood films, or films made by European directors working in America. Documentaries such as *The Plough that Broke the Plains* were sponsored by government agencies, not Hollywood studios. Although officially a Hollywood film in terms of its distribution, King Vidor's *Our Daily Bread* was essentially an independent film financed by individuals (including Vidor and D. W. Griffith) rather than by studios and banks. A remarkable documentary on wheat farming, the compact, one-reel *Forgotten Victory* was made by Germany's Fred Zinneman. *City Girl* was likewise made by a German, F. W. Murnau. And *the* classic among Hollywood films with an agricultural theme—*The Southerner* (based on the novel *Hold Autumn in Your Hand)*—was perhaps the best of a handful of films that Jean Renoir, the French director, made during his wartime exile in Hollywood. Although much more of a "story" film, it is the closest that Hollywood ever came to that "definitive" film about farming—the lovely, lyrical, and quite unforgettable French film *Farrebique.* Neither fiction nor documentary (though something of a forerunner of the *cinema verité* documentary), it is quite the best film about farm life ever made. Though its "stars" are the farm itself and the four seasons of the year, it has beauty, drama, pathos, even comedy. Although it celebrates a way of life that probably has passed into history (it was made in 1946), it can stand for all time as a testimonial to farming as a "calling." Would that Hollywood had made just *one* film that so celebrated and preserved on film the essence of American agricultural life.

Goin' to Jail

"Well, I guess I'm a goin' to Jail," Bill Bryan says
    when we meet on a Thursday in town.
"They keep sendin' me these government cattle census reports
    and tellin' me it's law number so and so I got to fill 'em out.
I guess I'm goin' to jail,
    cause I just throw 'em into the wastebasket.

There's already been two phone calls while I was at the ranch
    and I don't know how many while I wasn't.
This nice girl called and asked me how I could keep on ranching
    without the information in those cattle census reports.

I told her I really didn't know,
    but I'd been doin' it somehow for about 30 years.
I told her those cattle reports didn't mean too much
    cause no body ever put down anything
        that was true in 'em anyway.
Why if the cattle census taker, and the banker, and the tax man
    ever got together in the same room, we'd all be out of business.

Course those cattle census reports never
    include the summer or the winter rains either."

She said, Then just what do you base
    your business decisions on?

I said, What I got between my ears.
    I told her it wasn't much,
and it was wrong about 90% of the time,
    but at least it was mine.

She thanked me, and hung up.

Drum Hadley

Part Three
Food and Politics

Thadis W. Box is Dean of the College of Natural Resources in Utah State University. He has published widely in range management, especially in arid and semi-arid lands.

Loris Jones lives near Genesee, Idaho. She is the Agriculture Editor of the *Moscow Daily Idahonian*.

Burrt Trueblood farms near Homedale, Idaho. He co-chaired the Governor's Idaho Wildlife Tomorrow Conference in 1977.

M. Rupert Cutler is Assistant Secretary for Natural Resources and Environment, U.S. Department of Agriculture. He supervises the Soil Conservation Service, the Forest Service, and the Office of Environmental Quality.

Ray Jergesen is an author and lecturer.

Public Land Policy and Agriculture in the West

Thadis W. Box

Agriculture in the West is, and always has been, highly dependent upon the public lands. The small amounts of arable land that lie along the foothills and in the valleys depend upon the public lands for irrigation, forage for livestock, wood for construction, and other materials. And without the public lands, agriculture would never have been developed in those foothills. In more recent times it has been possible to transport wood and construction materials from other areas, but the agricultural land is still dependent on the adjoining lands for water, forage, and outdoor recreation.

Historically the development of our public-land policies can be divided into three major periods: *the era of development and exploitation, the era of preservation,* and *the era of reclamation and environmental control.* These eras roughly reflect national attitudes toward land, public and private. The eras are not distinct; they overlap. But each has had a definite impact upon the development and use of land both private and public.

From the time the first European settlers arrived in America, there has been an attempt to develop and exploit the land resource. Because land was cheap and considered almost inexhaustible, development and even exploitation, were thought to be good. The taming of the wilderness was a national goal. This era existed from the time of the first Europeans to the late nineteenth century.

After the settlement of California and the Civil War, people began to move into the undeveloped West. It was then that the scenic beauty of some areas prompted people to preserve the land.

[93]

National parks were set aside, the forest-reserve system was developed, and the general idea was established of preserving the land, or at least some of it, for public use.

As the land was settled, areas became overcut, overplowed, and overgrazed, and erosion and environmental degradation became widespread. Out of this pattern of overuse emerged a national objective: to reclaim the land. In the mid-1920s, even during the depth of the Depression, make-work projects were established to reclaim the land, the Soil Erosion Service was formed, the Taylor Grazing Act was implemented, and a number of attempts were made to reclaim what had been lost.

These eras were geared almost entirely to ownership: At first the attempt was to transfer individual blocks of land into private ownership; next the energy was directed toward saving the land from destruction by preserving it in public ownership. Then, out of the ferment of the 1960s, a whole new conservation movement arose; and it is in this era of environmental controls and environmental awareness that we live today.

Each era had a distinct impact on national policies toward federal lands, most of which were located in the West. When the first settlers arrived in most western states, the official policy of the United States was to move the land into private ownership as quickly and efficiently as possible. Various homestead acts were passed that would give a specific number of acres to individual citizens if they, in return, developed the land. In general these land policies were not suitable to the needs of the West. Some people, notably John Wesley Powell, wrote and argued at length that the West should be built around water, around drainage patterns or watersheds, and that large amounts of land should be used in common.

But Congressmen, executives, and bureaucrats who had been raised in the humid East, continued to parcel out land in square blocks. As homesteaders attempted to settle the land and in many cases failed, Congress, instead of completely reviewing the homestead acts, simply enlarged them. But each time they were enlarged, the maximum size remained too small for an economic unit to exist. Many laws, such as the Stock-raising Homestead Act of 1916, required that more animals be kept on the land than the land could sustain.

In addition, land was given to railroads for the construction of roads, and individual sections were given to the states for the construction of schools and for other purposes. The result is a land-ownership pattern in which the fertile areas along streams and around water are privately owned and the remainder of the state is a checkerboard of private, state, and federal blocks.

From about 1865 Congress began to set aside various portions of the public domain for scenic and other special uses. This concern for preservation dominated public-land policies for several years. The national park system was established first, beginning with Yellowstone, and gradually it expanded as other parks were added. Forest reserves were established around the turn of the century and were supplemented throughout the first third of the twentieth century. Next, wildlife refuges were established. Then, in an attempt to protect scenic and historic areas, areas of wildlife breeding, and valuable timber supply, Congress enacted policies that eventually would withdraw public land from consideration for private ownership. As a result, large areas of public land were set aside as parks, wildlife refuges, and so on. In addition, even larger areas, including the national forests, were withdrawn from consideration for private ownership.

The history of settlement in the West is one of immediate occupancy and exploitation. Records indicate that within two decades of settlement, the ranges around settlements in every area of the West were overgrazed. The results were erosion, salinization of soil, and other ills that often were incurable. The attitude that new land was available "over the hill" still dominated American thinking.

But when the widespread erosion and overuse caused dust storms on the plains and mud slides in the West, local citizenry took action. In the West new national forests were created and old ones expanded in an attempt to preserve the landscape. Some land in the public domain was transferred to Forest Service control; some private land was actually purchased and given to the Forest Service for management. A good case study is the Wellsville Mountains on the west side of Cache Valley in northern Utah. By the 1930s these mountains were so badly overcut and overgrazed that local rainstorms caused mud slides. The village water supply was being degraded and many stream channels endangered. Private landowners donated some land and raised money to purchase some, and they transferred the mountains to the Cache National Forest for management. Today the landscape is stable.

And now, these very lands—which only forty years ago were so degraded that private citizens gave them to the Forest Service— are being considered for wilderness designation. If land so degraded can be restored to wilderness condition in only four decades, wilderness is indeed a renewable resource, and the argument of many today that the huge areas of wilderness should continually be set aside to save them from us may not be valid.

The degraded condition of the land, coupled with the depressed economy of the 1930s, led to legislation creating makework projects, such as the Works Progress Administration and the Civilian Conservation Corps, to reclaim the land. It led also to the establishment of the Soil Erosion Service (later to become the Soil Conservation Service), the enactment of the Taylor Grazing Act, and the bringing of livestock grazing under control on the public domains. By World War II our country had gone through a complete cycle in attitudes toward the land: exploitation, to preservation, to reclamation. Public policies toward land had changed accordingly, but the object of each policy was to produce an effect on the land itself.

I maintain that the purpose of today's era of environmental control is slightly different. Today's attitudes and public policy are geared, not to the land, but to the survival of human beings and their aesthetic enjoyment of environment.

The environmental era began with the writings of such prophets and poets as David Thoreau, Aldo Leopold, and John Muir. The reverence for wilderness and nature became an obsession in the minds of a few. Then, following Rachel Carson's book *Silent Spring*, this obsession became the focus of coffee-table conversation nationwide.

The thought that we would not only lose our wilderness but would poison the cities and the countryside as well became a real national concern. This concern, tied to the Vietnamese war, and the general ferment of the 1960s, created a new allegiance to our environment. And even though this allegiance was not really tied to the land but to some vague idea of environmental pureness, a whole series of acts of Congress reflected concern for the environment. Beginning with the Wilderness Act in 1965, these acts dealt with the environment, clean water, clean air, surface mining, wild horses and burros, and the like. The most significant was probably the National Environmental Policy Act of 1969, which required a rather elaborate environmental-impact assessment of any significant action.

Collectively these laws expressed a national desire for a clean and livable environment, for saving what we have, a distrust of professional managers, and a desire to return to a vaguely defined concept of nature.

These statements of public-land policy were developed at a time of affluence and moral reexamination. The productivity of the land was secondary, the pioneer spirit of conquering land was rejected, and any technological solution to the problem was distrusted. In today's environment of high inflation, joblessness, and projected depression, the public attitude may change, but at least for the present we must deal with those expressions of public concern that have become part of our public policy.

Out of the ferment of the sixties came several statements of public-land policy that directly affect the West. They began in the late 1960s with the establishment of the Public Land Law Review Commission. Other commissions dealing with such subjects as recreation also published recommendations on the use of the public lands. Many of these recommendations were temporarily set aside during the troubles in Vietnam and Cambodia, but in the early 1970s Congress passed a series of acts dealing with land management.

The Resources Planning Act of 1974 required that the Forest Service assess the condition and potential of all noncultivated lands of the United States. The Resources Conservation Act next required the Soil Conservation Service to collect data on private land. Following were the National Forest Management Act of 1976, the Federal Land Management and Policy Act (commonly known as the BLM Organic Act), a rangeland-planning act, and other laws dealing with public lands. Amendments to bills currently in Congress would limit livestock reductions on public lands to a certain percentage point each year.

In the meantime, the courts have been brought into the action. A suit filed by the Natural Resource Defense Council against the Bureau of Land Management resulted in a settlement requiring that the BLM write environmental-impact statements on each of its grazing allotments. Suits now being filed challenge those environmental-impact statements, and the courts will again be asked to rule on individual cases.

Collectively recent laws say that public lands are important, that they will be kept in federal ownership, that they will be managed for multiple uses, that good science should be applied to the public lands, and that the agencies managing the public lands will be accountable for their actions. These statements reflect what the public, through their elected officials in Congress, have said about the public lands.

However, there are a number of minority opinions as to what is wanted and needed from the public lands. The two best expressions of these opinions, from the national executive section of our government and from western legislators, come down on different sides of the issue because they derive from different segments of the public.

The last several U.S. presidents have listened to environmentalists and responded to their demands. During President Ford's last month in office he attempted to double the size of the National Park and recreation lands. President Carter has used such vague authority as the Antiquity Act to set aside large amounts of land in Alaska and the West. And the RARE I and RARE II studies

(Forest Service attempts to inventory wilderness lands) are yet another example of the executive's listening to the environmentalists, recognizing the availability of votes there, and acting to set aside land for single uses.

On the other side of the ledger, in what is termed the "Sagebrush Rebellion," the legislatures of the western public-land states have reacted to the environmental movement and the executive actions. Reflecting local rather than national views, they indicate that they are being treated as colonies, that the eastern management does not understand their needs, and that they must assure their own futures by making decisions at the grass-roots level.

Both the actions of recent presidents and the demands expressed in the Sagebrush Rebellion reflect views of rather restricted audiences, but neither represents the views of the country as a whole. Imperfect though they may be, the laws coming out of Congress—the result of a long process of modification, of tradeoffs among various local groups in smoke-filled committee rooms, and of public debate on the floor—probably are the best reflection of the general national view.

In discussing public-land policies and the future of agriculture in the West, I will consider three scenarios: (1) the future of agriculture in the West if the present public policies continue, (2) what might happen to agriculture in the West if an extreme environmental posture is taken, and (3) what will happen if the proponents of private ownership of the public lands, as expressed in the Sagebrush Rebellion, prevail. In doing so I will use three criteria: the effect of public policy on water supply, on land available, and on animal agriculture, or grazing.

Finally, in analyzing the effects of public policy, I will make a number of assumptions. First is that the human population of the western states will continue to grow. Not only is the birth rate higher in the West than in the country as a whole, but it is an area of immigration. Second is that the energy resources of the West will be developed regardless of public-land policies, and that the development of this energy source will have a major effect on the use of agricultural land. Third is that the indicators of water supply, water availability, and grazing availability suggest the general state of agriculture. Nevertheless, I am fully aware that such things as quality of water, the national economy, and attitudes of local zoning boards may overshadow any specific scenario and may shift policies at any time.

If the present public policy on use and development of hydro-carbons and other energy-related minerals continues, they will be the primary factor affecting water supply and land use. As coal, oil-shale, and oil-and-gas leases are developed, more water will be demanded. The amount of water will depend upon the hydrocarbon selected and the kind of processing used. For instance, if *in situ* oil-shale and tar-sand processes succeed, the amount may be low. However, if these same products are brought to the surface and processed using systems that require heating, cooling, and physi-cally changing the raw material to another product, large amounts of water may be used. Certainly mine-mouth conversion plants for coal or slurry pipelines will use large amounts. In fact, any process used to convert energy resources into a form useful to the large population centers and then to transport the product to those cen-ters will require water.

Because most of the water has already been filed upon and is in use now, the major supply will be reallocated from agriculture. And the reduced availability of agricultural water will require changes in agricultural practices.

Present public-land policies also indicate that there will be less land available for agriculture. I do not mean to suggest that the public will be buying up private land, but as the pressures from immigration, energy development, and other industrial develop-ment increase in the West, the only land available for industrial plants, highways, housing, and other uses associated with industrial growth will be drawn from the agricultural base.

The public-land policies centering around grazing and animal agriculture have attracted much public attention in recent years. Hardly a newspaper in the West is now printed without some arti-cle on reduction in grazing privileges. Present land policies will result in a short-term lowering of the grazing use on public lands but will cause probably long-term stability and perhaps even an increase in use. The short-term lowering of grazing allowed on public lands will cause additional pressure on the private lands and could end up in a loss of midsized family-farm livestock opera-tions. There may be an increase in the number of small hobby farms and some consolidation of large economic operations. In sum, to-day's public-land policies will reduce agricultural productivity in the West.

If we take a second scenario, in which the public-land policies assume an extreme environmental posture, the effect on the future of agriculture is slightly different. For instance, extreme environmental pressures might stabilize the water supply by limiting energy development and industrial growth. Even so, it is doubtful that additional water would be available for agriculture, because most available water has already been filed upon, and under an extreme environmental scenario much more water would be reserved for in-stream uses, that is, for bird refuges, fish, and the like.

The extreme environmental approach probably would put more pressure on private land than do present policies. Uses of public lands would become more restricted, and many uses for which public land is now employed would have to be shifted to private land. This then would mean less land available for agriculture. The effects on animal agriculture would be even more severe. If the extreme environmental posture were assumed, grazing on public lands would be restricted, less land would be available, and little of the available land would be in close proximity to the family or small farm.

The result of this environmental posture would be an overall lowering of agricultural productivity, and a loss of midsized family farming operations, with an increase in the size and number of larger economic units.

The other extreme—a transfer of public lands into private ownership—would produce yet another effect on agriculture.

If all land were in private ownership, the availability of water for agriculture would decrease much more rapidly than under the other two scenarios. The mining industry would increase rapidly, energy development would be more rapid, the demand for water for these industries would increase, and water would shift through the market economy from agriculture to industry. The major difference between this scenario and the others would be the speed which water would be diverted from agriculture into industrial or culinary uses.

If all the public lands of the West were available for private ownership, the total amount of land available for private use would be increased substantially. It is uncertain, though, whether there would be more land available for agriculture. Some industrial development could be diverted to what is now public land, but because of the proximity of markets, transportation, and the like to agricultural land, it probably would continue to be adapted for other uses. Nevertheless, making public land available for private ownership should slow that trend considerably.

On first examination, one would assume that making public land available for private ownership would make more land available for animal production. However the assumption has dubious merit. For instance, many high-elevation pastures would be used for summer-home developments and private recreation. In addition, much lower-elevation land near the cities would shift from multiple-use grazing lands into small hobby farms and ranches. Much of what is now spring-fall grazing range for livestock and winter grazing range for big game could well become Shetland pony range.

The probable effects of moving land into private ownership would be a rapid loss of water, the hasty development of recreational properties and hobby farms, and an overall lowering of agricultural productivity in the West.

It is fairly safe to say that none of the above three scenarios will actually happen. It is unlikely that the present public-land policies will stand forever. It is equally improbable that the environmentalists will capture and rule the country, or that our public lands will be sold and converted to private ownership. The pattern probably will be a general, slow modification of current public-land policies. Federal and state governments will respond piecemeal to the national and regional demands for more energy, recreation, and other products of public lands and in so doing will subvert the long-range planning that Congress has required in the Resources Planning Act, the National Forest Management Act, and the Federal Land Management and Policy Act. There will be continual attempts to modify public-land policies by executive order or state legislative action, but these efforts will have little long-term effect. It is the will of the people, imperfectly translated through their elected Congressmen, that will enable us to continue muddling through public-land management policies one issue at a time.

So what is the future of agriculture in the West? Unfortunately, regardless of what scenarios are followed, there will be less available land and water and reduced productivity. This lowering of productivity will not necessarily be a function of the land itself or of our ability to manage the land; rather, it will be a function of the growth rate (which is higher in the West than in the nation as a whole) and of the availability of land. However, this trend is no cause for alarm. We now import our food from other areas, and in the future we will simply increase our dependence on the more productive lands of California and the Midwest and will produce what we can provide most readily: recreation, energy, feeder livestock, and wildlife.

Agricultural Research

Loris Jones

If U.S. farmers are expected to be the ultimate source of food for the world, they must have plant varieties that can produce the needed grains, fruits, and vegetables.

The nation's land-grant colleges and universities play a vital role in the effort to keep producers supplied with high-yielding plants, as do many seed companies. But it isn't a one-time achievement. The effort must continue, because many plant varieties seem to fade or lose their productive capacity, succumbing to various insects or diseases. New plants are needed that can provide forage for meat animals on land unsuitable for other kinds of agriculture.

Therefore, agricultural research, whether funded privately or by federal and state governments, is vitally important to the future, not only of the Rocky Mountain West, but of all the country—indeed, of the world.

However, in the effort to balance the federal budget, agricultural research funds have been cut drastically, and, to quote Assistant Secretary of Agriculture Rupert Cutler, "If you think it's bad this year, wait until next year." Idaho recently passed a property tax limit; subsequently, the legislature has eliminated two research programs at the University of Idaho and cut back other research funds. This behavior seems to me to be very short-sighted, in view of the world's increasing population and in view of the gradual take-over of farm land by roads, houses, industrial plants, and other urban developments.

Not only does the farmer need new plant varieties to guarantee adequate food production; he or she needs methods to control insects and diseases that threaten food crops. As an example, in Idaho and California researchers are working to find a natural enemy of rush skeletonweed, a pest that is taking over vast areas of rangeland in both states, and in Washington State. A second example: In northern Idaho, dry peas are an important crop. However, acres of Austrian winter peas have been sharply reduced because of a disease that decimated the plants, cutting yields to uneconomic levels. In the past four years another pest—the pea-leaf weevil—has caused consternation among pea growers who produce special seed for national soup companies and for canning and freezing. Because no natural enemy has been found for these pea-leaf weevils, growers must rely on chemical controls—an expensive procedure.

This points up another problem faced by farmers everywhere: growing public opposition to the use of chemicals in agriculture. Somehow we must find ways to reduce chemical use while maintaining production—a feat that can be accomplished only through research.

Typically the public is unaware of the importance of agricultural research, even though that research can increase the variety and reduce the cost of foods.

Research and the Strength of Our Agriculture

Burrt Trueblood

In 1964, having raised our family in Alaska, we came back to Idaho and started farming on the family homestead. We tried to raise alfalfa seed using the technique that had been successful when we were kids. It was a total failure. That first year we had a hundred and forty pounds to the acre. It was a disaster simply because there were no pollenizers. Alfalfa is unique in that the honey bee is a very unsuccessful pollenizer for it. Honey-bee activity might produce a hundred pounds to the acre. The most effective bee, one that also is native to the area, is the alkali bee. While we were gone, the alkali bees completely disappeared. I have no idea what happened to them. I heard that they were killed by improper use of insecticides that had been developed directly after World War II.

So we began using the alfalfa leaf-cutting bee, an exotic import into the United States that, through proper management, is proving quite successful. The management of this species was taught to us primarily by the University of Idaho Extension Service people, and the research was done by the Extension Service and later by the alfalfa seed growers' organizations, which finance much of the current research.

In the western states we have a massive research program focusing on the alfalfa leaf-cutting bee. It is too big for an individual grower by himself. In California, Nevada, Washington, Utah, and Idaho researchers are studying pollenizers.

It is frightening to see federal funding being cut off from these programs. And the Carter Administration is cutting agricultural research severely. The Office of Management and Budget is substituting short-term programs for long-term programs. They are looking for results within three to five years.

It took twenty-eight years of research to develop the first short-stem, high-yield dwarf wheat, which in turn led to the Green Revolution. Today's OMB funding would never have supported such a program.

Private business is doing a great deal in funding research, but just the same they think twice about a program that takes as long as wheat development. It takes a combination of growers, educational facilities, and federal funding—the whole works—because you cannot learn much in any given year.

We have put money into alkali bees, trying to reintroduce them into the area. Our leaf-cutter bees are not as strong as they were. Many different problems show up every year with them. Because it is an exotic, the leaf cutter is subject to new problems. But we are keeping up with the necessary research.

If we had not produced alfalfa seed in Canyon County and Treasure Valley, Idaho, and in two or three special areas in Washington, California, and Nevada, the alfalfa seed would have had to be grown in the Midwest. But in Oklahoma it would require ten acres to produce as much alfalfa seed as we get from one acre here. So the efficiency of our production is one reason to protect it and is one reason why this region is unique.

The Carter Administration's attitude toward the financing of agricultural research and agricultural conservation is heart-sickening. Countries rise and fall with the strength of their agriculture. And we in the United States are likewise dependent on the vitality of our agriculture. We must begin now to preserve it.

Rocky Mountain Agriculture: Abundant or Depleted?

M. Rupert Cutler

It is clear to me that a continuing, viable agriculture in the Rocky Mountains is fully in the nation's interest. The topics of the major sessions of the FARM symposium—physical resources, human resources, and food and politics—cover well the elements essential to the future of agriculture.

The U.S. Department of Agriculture is in full accord with the policy of having decisions on agriculture in the Rockies made by and with the people who live here.

The shape of agriculture in the Rocky Mountain states has been forged by three controlling types of physical resources: the dominating mountains, the life-giving rivers, and the interspersed valleys and extensive plains.

To the uninformed and inexperienced, massive mountain ranges are symbols of rugged durability and changelessness. But to those who know, these peaks are brittle and crumbly and are constantly undergoing change wrought by wind, water, avalanches, and earthquakes. The changes run from miniscule to catastrophic, but all are important. All affect the delicate balance of existence for plants and animals adapted to the shallow soils and alpine terrain. In addition there are man-made changes. Earth-gouging machines can strip away the thin layer of soil on a mountainside, leaving gaping sores that fester through erosion. Exploitative cutting of timber on steep slopes likewise erodes mountainsides and fills streams with silt.

Water from the mountains always has been the key to agriculture in the Rockies. Without water, people and livestock have died, and crops have dried up and blown away. But even in the best of Rocky Mountain locations, water always has been a limited resource.

Arid and semiarid valleys and plains form the foundation for a ranching/farming agriculture. In the early days Indians and Spaniards found whole valleys and plains to their liking. And then the sons and daughters of New England fled from small, stone-fenced farmsteads to the expansive, open slopes of the Rockies.

Mountains, water, valleys and plains—the physical resources that determine the agriculture of the Rocky Mountains. It is no wonder that issues regarding these often explode into flaming controversy. And among the physical-resource issues that demand solution, water—for irrigation, energy, and range—heads the list.

Irrigated agriculture in the eight Rocky Mountain states includes more than a fourth of the irrigated farms and 30 percent of the irrigated acres in the United States. Nevada and Arizona have little if any nonirrigated cropland. Better than 80 percent of the value of crops produced in Utah, Idaho, Wyoming, and New Mexico comes from irrigated lands. Colorado has the largest irrigated acreage of the Rocky Mountain states, and that land produces over half of Colorado's crops.

With or without statistics, it is obvious that agriculture in the Rockies would scarcely exist except for irrigation. This is true whether we are talking about flooding a hay meadow with water from Troublesome Creek in Colorado or irrigating citrus and date trees with water carried through sophisticated diversion and conveyance systems from the Salt River in Arizona.

It would be a gross understatement to characterize water for irrigation in the Rocky Mountains as a limited resource. At times it is downright scarce. Since the supply, primarily from snow melt, cannot be controlled, there are only two choices for ensuring enough for the future. We can either limit demand or conserve use.

Limiting demand for water sometimes seems about as feasible as slowing an avalanche. For example, water consumption for agriculture from the Yellowstone River is expected to increase by 45 percent in the next twenty years. An estimate for the Upper Colorado region projects an increase of 25 percent. Use of water for electrical power and mining will more than triple.

The greatest threat to water supplies comes, however, from the downriver demand of population centers and future growth of synfuel production. Although the burgeoning population and industrial development of California is a major source of concern to water-conscious people in the Rockies, they don't have to look that far away to find a problem. The Rockies have their own expanding centers, where masses of people water their lawns and refill their swimming pools, and industries guzzle enormous amounts of water that could be growing crops.

The controversial competition between upriver and downriver uses is an old story to those who live in the Rockies. They reduced these difficultues within agriculture by creating laws that establish senior and junior appropriators of water and other regulations. And to deal with the complex interstate traverse of the rivers, they developed a number of interstate compacts or requested court apportionment of water supply.

These laws and compacts are essential to the orderly allocation of water uses. However, as new demands arise and traditional ones increase, the existing regulations must be examined critically and modified as needed to prevent their becoming barriers to the maintenance of a strong agriculture.

The development of the synfuel industry is a good example. President Carter has committed his administration to an all-out effort to make this country self-sufficient in energy resources by 1990. And one of the primary means for achieving this goal is the development of oil-shale deposits. An adequate supply of water exists in the Upper Colorado basin, but there is a mismatch between the location of the richest and largest oil-shale deposits, in northwestern Colorado, and the location of the greatest amount of unused water, in northeastern Utah and southwestern Wyoming.

Therefore, unless costly aqueducts bring in surplus water from adjoining subbasins, the oil-shale industry must depend on unused local water. To do so means buying water rights—most of which are now used for agriculture. Unlimited purchase of surface water rights for an industry using two million barrels per day could withhold water from 20 percent of the acreage currently irrigated in the oil-shale regions. Industry needs for surface water could be reduced initially by using groundwater, but because surface and ground flows are connected, eventually both would be depleted.

Similar competition for water will increase between agriculture and developing fuel industries in the Yellowstone Basin. Withdrawals of Yellowstone water for industry could far exceed the 350,000–450,000 acre-feet estimated to be available above instream needs and existing consumption. Additional impoundments or new interbasin aqueducts will be expensive. Groundwater from aquifers is fully committed, and potential supplies from the deep Madison Aquifer are highly variable.

In the face of this threat to Rocky Mountain agriculture, local, state, and federal people and agencies must work together closely. But beyond the question of retaining agriculture's share of water in the Rocky Mountains, there is much to gain from conserving both water and energy.

The major water losses from off-farm conveyance systems result from seepage through unlined canals and through cracks and breaks in lined canals and from operational spills caused by poor system design or management. Other off-farm losses come from excessive vegetative growth in and adjacent to canals. The major losses on-farm result from surface runoff, deep percolation of applied irrigation water, and seepage from unlined field ditches.

The recent interagency report entitled "Irrigation Water Use and Management" estimates the potential savings from a comprehensive irrigation-water conservation program in seventeen western states. As an example, for the mountain areas of Colorado, Wyoming, Montana, Idaho, and New Mexico, the reduction of consumption losses could make 300,000 acre-feet available for other uses. Canal and ditch lining, both off- and on-farm, along with changes in method and land leveling on-farm, are the most important means for reducing loss. However, the off-farm measures would be nearly twice as costly as on-farm measures, and although there would be dollar savings overall, the benefits to ranchers and farmers would not always be sufficient to justify the use of private capital.

In the lower valleys and plains, improvements would include canal lining, consolidation, realignment, and enlargement of off-farm installations. Automation, ditch lining, land leveling, tailwater recovery systems, and control structures are important on-farm measures. Savings to farmers would result from reduced pumping, and as energy prices rise, the dollar savings would increase.

I have discussed at length the quantity of water supplies. However, water quality is equally important, not only for agriculture but also for other uses. It is well known that the concentration of soil constituents in irrigation water degrades the quality of that water. In addition, reduced streamflow conditions and unscreened irrigation diversions adversely affect fisheries, wildlife, and recreation.

On the other hand, increased efficiency in irrigation systems can further degrade water quality. The seepage from off- and on-farm distribution systems has created habitats for many forms of fish and wildlife, and reducing or eliminating that seepage can destroy that habitat. Therefore, we must accelerate our use of substitutes for fossil-fuel energy. We can increase the use of organic wastes and legumes as fertilizer. We have a real opportunity to increase energy production from biomass, particularly from forest residues and other timber not suitable for lumber or pulp. We can continue to expand our uses of active and passive solar systems. We can multiply our current use of wind power and low-head hydro-power. Much of the technology to exploit these opportunities is already available. However, with additional research, there is potential for major increases in efficiency.

As with water, conservation of energy is a vital key to keeping costs down. Preventing soil erosion and thus maintaining yields is a major means of saving energy. Similarly, preservation of prime farmland can provide long-term energy savings. Windbreaks and shelterbelts in the plains can help save energy in heating farm homes, removing snow, feeding livestock, and producing crops. Increased rangeland productivity can reduce the need for grains that have high-energy requirements for their production.

But for Rocky Mountain agriculture the improvement of rangelands is important for more reasons than simply potential energy savings. The Rocky Mountain states contain 60 percent of the nation's rangeland and 30 percent of the grazed forest land, and a recent study within the U.S. Department of Agriculture indicates that the ever-growing demand for red meat over the next fifty years could increase by 36 percent the demand for range grazing in the Rocky Mountain states. In addition, the rangelands of ten western states provide forage for an estimated sixty-three thousand wild horses and burros. And the big-game population of seven Rocky Mountain states totals more than two million.

In addition to forage, the rangelands supply coal, oil, uranium, and other minerals. They also provide sites for many forms of outdoor recreation, such as hunting, hiking, off-road vehicle use, and rockhounding.

Some old and well-established range uses are growing in importance, too. The harvesting of pinyon nuts, once largely an activity of only a few Indian tribes in the Southwest, now is a popu-

lar recreation activity for many people. Juniper has traditionally
provided fence posts and (along with pinyon) firewood for ranchers.
But now, with rising fuel costs, urban dwellers also are demanding
juniper and pinyon for use as fuel. In some areas the demands are
so great that supplies must be managed closely.

Finally, the challenge to established uses of rangelands will
increase if the development of certain specialty crops proves feasible. The production of guayule for rubber, Euphorbia for petroleum, and jojoba for industrial oil could involve millions of arid
rangeland acres in New Mexico, Arizona, and other southwestern
states.

If we are to meet all these demands for range, we must improve the productivity of these lands. The USDA intends to help
bring that about. In October 1980 Secretary of Agriculture Bob
Bergland signed a departmental policy memorandum on range
improvement. Called a "Statement of Range Policy," it is the first
of its kind in the USDA. It calls for increased cooperation and coor-
dination with federal, state, and private organizations, institutions,

and individuals on range programs. Agencies are to improve the quality of their service to range owners and users. They are to accelerate the conservation and improvement of range resources and are to prevent duplication and overlap of activities. Emphasis also is to be placed on strong research, extension, and technical-assistance programs. Additional emphasis is to be given to financial assistance through loans and cost sharing.

The agencies in the USDA have been asked to respond to the requirements of this new policy memorandum within the next year.

Although water, energy, and rangeland represent the major physical-resource issues in the future of Rocky Mountain agriculture, we should not overlook the forest lands. In this region, forest and agricultural lands are not really separable; they overlap and intermingle, so that the management of one affects the management of the other. What happens to the forest affects the quantity and quality of water for agriculture. What happens to range grazing affects the regrowth of forests.

The new policy memo establishes a department-wide Committee on Range Policy cochaired by the director of Science and Education, Dr. Anison Bertrand, and myself. (Incidentally, Dr. Bertrand is a Texan, the former dean of agriculture at Texas Tech University at Lubbock, and a range-management authority.) The committee's job will be to find practical ways to implement Secretary Bergland's policy directive. These include more assistance to range owners applying range-conservation treatments, financial assistance to young farmers and ranchers, and credit opportunities to grazing associations.

The committee also is to work on arid- and semiarid-land lines with Mexico, develop IPM approaches for rangeland, and help define the federal role in the management of predators on public land. Both are important to the fish and wildlife of the area.

Like water, energy, and rangelands, the forest lands are faced with mounting demands for multiple uses. Consequently, without increased forest productivity, this country will not be able to meet the timber demands of the future. Nevertheless, by undertaking intensive management practices, we can increase the productivity of national and private commercial forests. However, the greatest potential for increased productivity is in farm and other private nonindustrial forest lands. We must learn how to unlock the potential of all the forest resources.

When increasing forest productivity, we also must meet public needs for recreation, wilderness, livestock forage, and other uses. To do this for the national forests, the USDA engaged in a nation-wide assessment of forest resources and developed policies for achieving important national goals. And in January 1980 President Carter recommended to Congress a national forest policy based on the Forest and Range Resources Planning Act (RPA). He addressed the issues of what we need, how to meet these needs, and how to handle the inherent tradeoffs among timber and nontimber values.

The issue of public ownership of land in the Rocky Mountains and the rest of the West overrides all four physical-resource issues I have mentioned. All eight states contain huge acreages of public domain. For example, the federal government owns nearly a third of the land in Montana and nearly seven-eighths of the land in Nevada. The other six states are in between. And everyone knows that he who owns the land controls the resources.

The dominant federal presence in these states tends to distort normal federal-state-private landholder relations. That is, as the population of the Rocky Mountain area grows, people find themselves crowding, not only each other, but more often than not, the ever-present federal boundaries.

More than that, people are constantly hitting snags on one or more of the innumerable federal, state, and local regulations regarding water, land, environment, grazing, forestry, and energy.

A recent letter to Secretary Bob Bergland from a lady in Colorado typifies the feelings of many in the Rocky Mountains toward their encroaching neighbors and the federal government. She told him that she had written to the President and that the people in USDA were the last ones she wanted to deal with. Her problem was with a ditch owned by someone else and abutting her farm. In cleaning the ditch, the owners had dug it deeper than necessary for the adjudicated amount of water.

As a result, she can't get across the ditch. Beyond that, the bank erosion is undermining a pipe from a spring she owns on the upper side of the ditch. The result is that her spring water runs into the ditch instead of where she wants it. And the erosion is causing landslides and threatening to cut her land in two.

She wants help. She said the Soil Conservation Service couldn't do anything for her. She wouldn't deal with the Forest Service. (She had had to use a lot of money stopping them from getting three entrances to her land for an oil company. She hired a lawyer, but he didn't help her. He just took her money.) She had only the President to turn to for help, and she was going to write him again.

This letter is only one of hundreds we receive. Some are more sophisticated than others. But all have one thing in common: They are trying to cope with the local adjustments required by the disruptions that come with rapid change. They are frustrated by the presence of federal lands, federal laws, and federal rules. They have no control over a part of their environment—publicly owned land. They are affected by policies and decisions on that land, but they cannot anticipate them.

These deep feelings of frustration, regimentation, and helplessness strongly bias people against constructive improvements for Rocky Mountain agriculture. The outgrowths of these feelings are extreme: rebellion and resignation. And in between are all degrees of discouragement. These feelings block rational approaches to the problems of water supplies, energy, range, and forestry.

The federal government has an obligation to do something about providing elbow room for self-determination in the development of the Rocky Mountain Region. But giving all the public land back to the states or to private owners is not a real answer. The resources of the Rockies cannot be managed from within political boundaries. Nor does anyone believe that complete private ownership will provide the degree of stewardship required to maintain these resources for future generations.

However, there is room for more cooperative effort among the federal, state, and local jurisdictions and the people themselves. Certainly there is an urgent need for more public participation in decision-making on federal lands, particularly for decisions that affect people in the same area. (We know that the amount of citizen litigation intended to block unacceptable decisions is directly related to opportunities for public participation.) Consequently, President Carter has asked that all federal agencies improve their decision-making for significant program actions. And Secretary Bergland issued a memorandum calling for greater involvement of the public in our significant decisions. All decisions of USDA Forest Supervisors that affect nonfederal people are subject to administrative review. And in response to the RPA, which requires public participation, the Forest Service conducted a massive public-participation effort while developing its RARE I recommendations for wilderness and nonwilderness. (They received more than 250,000 responses.)

Similarly, the planning by the Soil Conservation Service, in accord with the Soil and Water Resources Conservation Act (RCA), will include extensive public participation. Every new national forest land-use plan will be based in part on public involvement. Last month citizens on the Front Range of Colorado, in cooperation with the Forest Service, completed a successful pilot project on controlling the mountain pine beetle. Private ownership held 44 percent of the 34,000 acres in the project. Sixteen residential subdivisions and four to five thousand people were involved. From all reports the support and cooperation between private landowners and the Forest Service was excellent. Infested trees were removed, forest stands thinned, the threat of uncontrolled wildfire reduced, fuel wood made available to meet energy needs, and the scenic quality of the area restored.

The processes the USDA has developed for public participation are based on the best available methodology and experience. This is not, however, to say that current procedures are the best for every need. We know that public participation must be adapted to the special needs of people in specific regions and also to the requirements of specific activities.

Therefore, the USDA is pledged to work with the public in developing means for increasing public participation in decisions of the Forest Service and the SCS.

There is some feeling that more agencies should be involved, but starting with these two might facilitate the development of a pattern for use with others. Furthermore, the Forest Service and the SCS represent two extremes in federal presence. (One is a large landholder; the other is entirely a service organization.)

The physical resources of the Rocky Mountains are among the most valuable and at the same time most vulnerable in the nation. But now a host of opportunities for improving the management of the resources will extend the benefits of those resources to future generations.

If these benefits are to be realized, representatives of the people must join with local, state, and federal governments in developing the necessary policies and decisions. That will be no easy task. But a person who senses the magnificence of this region, the dedication of the people in it, and its potential for improvement, must conclude that there is no goal more worthy of the effort.

Economic Realities

Ray Jergeson

In any economic structure one operates with a set of assumptions. The most basic is that producers must have a market return at least equal to the cost of production. Those family farms remaining are of value—culturally, socially, and in many other ways—but they can remain and be responsible to those values only through an economic equation that includes the cost of production plus a reasonable profit.

We all realize that every social order depends in some way on its agriculture. And each relationship between the order and the land is unique. For our own social order the fundamental question is this: Who should produce the food—our most basic energy? The poll in Idaho, I think, makes that very clear.[1] The next most important question follows: Is there any danger that the production of this basic energy will become as controlled and concentrated as is the production of petroleum energy?

I pose these questions as a backdrop to my discussion of economic reality.

The Grapes of Wrath etched our national consciousness, perhaps for all time. But because we see or read about no comparable farm exodus today, we assume that there is a greater degree of security among farm families. Statistics, however, point out the error in that assumption. Unlike the visible streams of humanity leaving rural America in the thirties, unlike the vocal and highly publicized milk dumpers of the fifties, today's farmers, when faced with economic ruin, leave quietly, selling out to a neighbor or to

[119]

a distant corporation. This very week two thousand are thus quietly leaving. In round figures what remains is a million farmers who raise 89 percent of all our production and 1.7 million who raise the remaining 11 percent. The latter group consists mainly of part-time or hobby farmers. For every dollar the full-time farmers made *on* the farm last year, the hobbyists made $1.52 *off* the farm. Frank LeRoux, economist and farmer from Walla Walla, points out in his latest published research, *The Myth of Agricultured Prosperity*, that farmers are in worse economic shape now than they were in the 1930s—given debt ratios, parity ratios, return of investment—given almost any economic measurement.[2] The government's own parity ratios of 15 September 1979 worked out as follows: wheat, 64 percent of parity; corn, 59 percent; pork, 52 percent; soybeans, 67 percent; all beef, 92 percent; lambs, 80 percent; barley, 61 percent; cotton, 58 percent; and milk, 74 percent.

It would seem we have always had a farm problem. Certainly my own recollections of growing up south of Chinook, Montana, are filled with discussions and endless meetings about the farm problem. The central problem, of course, was that we were going broke or continually borrowing more against steadily inflating land values. The various and particular experts had several answers to our questions—answers that usually boiled down to (1) get bigger, (2) get more efficient, or (3) get into another line of work. (Of course, Wendell Berry effectively examines and punctures each of those answers and more in his book *The Unsettling of America*.[3]) We were also told such fundamental truths as, "The world cannot pay more than $1.25 per bushel for wheat," and, "Canada undersells our market."

However, in the end everyone attending these meetings shrugged and suggested that it was all very complex and too bad. We left with our own sense of anxiety, concern, or downright fear, vowing to work harder and learn more about the latest wonders of agricultural technology and chemical use and about the various low-interest financing plans and other government programs that might be available and might even be explicable. Then we would get bigger. And today my own family, for example, farms what five families farmed forty years ago.

But we, like virtually all farmers, missed something essential: We missed examining our own behavior in the economic structure, and we missed examining the market system itself. As a result, I believe that farmers themselves are responsible for the sorry state of the agricultural economy.

To explain that, I will begin with the market system, and I will concentrate on grain (my most immediate specialty, you might say). But what I say is largely applicable to other commodities.

It goes without saying that we live in a world of systems. In my graduate-school days we were fond of shouting that the system was the problem. (Ma Bell, of course, countered with nationwide advertisements that the system was the solution.) The truth is that any system can function only according to its design and purpose. Thus, the judicial system is to decide right and wrong, and the educational system is to enlighten the citizens, generally the young. Neither of these systems, for example, was designed to move mail. That is the purpose of the postal system—a good reminder, I suppose, that some systems work better than others.

If we then study the traditional grain-procurement system, name its parts, see what it does, how it functions, and finally why it functions, we will be able to put our market system in perspective. We shall touch briefly upon each of those points.

The traditional grain-procurement system is everything beyond the farm gate: the local handlers and brokers (usually of the county level), the transportation components of the system beyond the farm, the major multinational firms (dominated by five private companies worldwide), and finally the domestic and foreign users— the feeders, millers, and grinders. The system includes neither the producer nor the consumer. This system is complemented, often directly affected, by any number of influences, such as speculators' position or government policy. When I exclude the farmer and the consumer from that system, I am reminded of the results of the Idaho poll: Sixty-seven percent of the respondents said they would be willing to pay 5 percent more for their food if that meant maintaining the family farm.[4] The fact is that even if 100 percent felt that way, it would have absolutely no effect on the Chicago market today. In the end the entire system that I have mentioned here— local brokers and handlers, the transporters, the corporate heads, and the major users have only one purpose: to move tremendous tonnage all over the world in response to continuing, increasing, and changing demand. The system has no other reason for existence.

The system protects itself and its purpose with low prices— in direct response to the behavior of farmers. Low prices do several things. First, they promote enormous production and continuous effort to increase that production. It motivates farmers to "mine" the land, to raise the best—or the most—per unit. We farmers are used to sitting around the fire winters, spitting at the coals, bragging about how much we raised. Low prices promote continuing research. Low prices force nearly every bushel into the market every year. (Simple mathematics, for example, show that it takes twice as many $2.50 bushels to pay the bills as it would take with $5 bushels.) And the system, which relies upon USDA projections (e.g., planted acres times normal yield) is perennially convinced that there is plenty of supply. In other words, the system assumes that every visible bushel is available and that it will be available in the same percentages to the same buyers as in any previous year.

The actual day-to-day competition is always downward. For example, if tonight Japan tenders 100,000 metric tons of red wheat for delivery next spring, the export company quoting the lowest price for the spring delivery will get the business. It should be no surprise that Japan, or any other purchaser, wants to buy as cheaply as possible. We all try to purchase on that basis.

At the time of the sale in this example, the grain trader will purchase a comparable futures contract to hedge against price fluctuation. The trader knows how farmers react to markets: Only 3 percent sell on the up market, and never the same 3 percent. The goal of every producer is to sell 100 percent of his crop at the top of the market. But because we don't control the market, we have to wait until it falls to find out where the top was. Apparently the 3 percent sell on the up market because they have bills to pay. That is, tomorrow a note is due. It's never the same 3 percent. And 7 percent sell after the break in the market. The other 90 percent sell in the so-called slough, the down market. Thus, two-thirds of all production is sold on the bottom third of the market. When wheat hit $6.40 a couple of years ago, we liked to sit around the fire again in the winter and brag about how we'd sold that whole crop at $6.40. But statistics show that less than one-half of one percent was sold at that figure. We are, after all, human. On the up market we hold; on the down, we panic and dump.

In 1972 our economic world and the confusion surrounding it changed our lives. The Russian wheat sale was only one factor behind that change. The devaluation of the dollar was only one factor. (For example, by the time our market hit $5 a bushel in U.S.

currency, it was costing the Japanese only $3.60 because of devaluation.) The Nixon Administration's response—ordering in all Commodities Credit Corporation (CCC) stocks—was another factor. This was a period of violent fluctuations. The system was in chaos. Before June 1973, grain traders had been able to buy CCC stocks to fill their commitments if farmers were not selling fast enough. Then, in June 1973, the traders found their *entire* source of supply, their lifeblood, in the hands of an unpredictable, unorganized, and undisciplined mob—farmers. These producers fell into three categories: (1) those who had sold all their production to pay immediate bills, as always, (2) those who, for whatever reason, had sold only enough to pay immediate bills and had gone fishing—who were paying no attention to the market, and (3) a large group who let greed take over and refused to sell because, in their minds, no matter where the market was, it was not yet good enough. In other words, we had $6 wheat but wanted $7. The lesson then was clear: High prices jeopardized the functioning of the system.

Three laws of systems had been or were simultaneously at work. First, any group without a system of its own is doomed to serve that of another. Farmers had not designed the primary system —never had anything but the most peripheral input. Prices are set by those with the knowledge and power to set them. Farmers had never exercised their respective power. The second law of the system is as follows: When any system fails, there will be chaos unless there is an alternative system to fall back upon. In politics, for example, if the Republicans stink a little too much, we hang them out to dry and try on the Democrats. There we have an alternative. But farmers failed to implement any alternative to the primary system. Third, and most important in system law: *When any group controls a commodity or service necessary to an essential industry but refuses to contract for orderly delivery at fair profit levels, they will find that basic commodity forced out of them by repressive means.* Farmers refused to contract fair-profit prices. Consequently, the industry had no choice but to work the direction downward. That is, the price had to be forced down to renew the flow of the system's lifeblood. And it happened. It took only one year, 1974, to put the cattle producers back in their cage. It took only three years to do the same with grain farmers. And it was done simply—the system and its components worked according to design. There was no need for a conspiracy. Questions of conspiracy between traders and government officials make for interesting study, but they are entirely moot.

Farmers' reactions were mixed. But overall their behavior resembled that of an alcoholic. First, they refused to admit that there was an economic problem. After all, everyone, even the Secretary of Agriculture, had assured them that they lived in the best of all possible worlds, that the market dives and plunges were just enough bad in this best of all possible worlds to remind one of how good the best really was. But that argument tarnished pretty badly when interior wheat prices fell to $1.85 a bushel. After all, export tonnage and domestic use were continuing to rise. Then, once farmers admitted the problem, often at the urging of their frightened lenders, they again reacted with an alcoholic's reasoning. They wanted to blame everyone and everything else. Surely it was the fault of the Secretary of Agriculture or of someone labeled "Government." Surely it was the fault of the press. Certainly it must be the fault of the futures market. If only the consumers knew. And what about the big companies? Surely they must have some responsibility. It was easy to blame everyone else for one's economic woes. And I too felt that urge to cast the blame.

But calculated analysis kept bringing us back to human behavior and system design. There were and no excuses.

What I am suggesting—and this might explain in part why I work every day organizing for collective bargaining—is that farmers have not only the total production responsibility, but also the task of assuring their economic survival. No other group even stands a remote chance of assuring that goal for farmers.

The overall economic facts are staggering. Our balance of trade suffers at least $2.8 billion because wheat is leaving the nation altogether too cheaply. For total grains—and there are some 12 billion bushels produced annually in this country—local economies are short-changed $24 billion. If you accept the five times multiple that raw materials generate as they move through the economy, the total economic effect is a loss of $120 billion.

Finally, if farmers cannot survive the economics, it will be impossible to resolve most other issues of rural America. Without farmers as we understand them (that is, as family units), the basis for discussing those issues changes so radically as to put us into uncharted territory.

No Cure for Cowboys

Where there's mountains, and deserts, and canyon country,
   and cows, and steers a runnin'—
There'll always be cowboys a whoopin', and a hollerin',
   whoooo ha, hid a, turn 'em down, head 'em,
drivin' 'em across the arroyos, and the canyons,
   drivin' 'em on down the valleys to home.

    "There's no cure for cowboys," Bill Bryan says.
      "Just look at these fellers livin' around here.
    They've tried weldin', minin', drivin' trucks,
      pumpin' gas, and all of 'em go back to a ranch
    somewheres, workin' for less than they could make
      most anyplace else they tried,
    or runnin' a few cows and steers, and losin' their shirts
      when the rains don't come, or the price drops—

    And when they aren't off on that ranch, they've got
      a horse out back of their house in town,
    and haul him off to a rodeo, or a ropin' most every weekend.
      They've got it in their hearts. They can't help it."

    Nope, there's no cure for cowboys.

Drum Hadley

Part Four

The Sagebrush Rebellion

David H. Leroy is the Attorney General of Idaho. He has published several articles and books on criminal liability, trials, and tactics.

Cecil D. Andrus is Secretary of the Interior. He was formerly the Governor of Idaho.

Gary Wicks is Director of the Bureau of Land Management for the State of Utah.

A Plea for Partnership

David H. Leroy

In discussing the Sagebrush Rebellion, it is important to establish what it is and what it is not in the West because there is a good deal of misperception about it. It is a frustration with federal government and land-management practices. It is a political battle that has been joined in Nevada, Oklahoma, California, Utah, Alaska, and Oregon. And shortly, I suppose with the coming of next season's legislatures, Wyoming, New Mexico, Arizona, and Idaho will enter the fray. In some sense it is a bit of a public-relations hype. And on the horizon is a legal battle: It is the legal aspect of ownership and federal-management practices that the Nevada legislation was designed to test. At this moment, however, there is no Nevada test case, no Nevada lawsuit or litigation involving that state's statute, which is the forerunner of the movement. In sum, the Sagebrush Rebellion is a revolution whose first shot has yet to be fired.

On the other hand, the Sagebrush Rebellion is not, and does not pretend to be, a panacea for all the ills in the clash between states' sovereignty and federal land management in the West. It is not a single legislative concept; at this count there are at least five concepts in several states, and probably by next year, when the issue is joined in the legislatures of the West, there will be at least fifty concepts of what the Sagebrush Rebellion is all about.

It is also fair to observe that at this point the Sagebrush Rebellion has no single, well-defined set of objectives. Some people see it as the states' attempt to take over certain types of federally owned lands—a battle to be fought in the courts or in the legislature. Others

view it as simply a vehicle to force a test case. And for still others, it
is intended to induce Congress to effect a gradual transfer of federal
lands to the states—in other words, to cause an honest reimple-
mentation of the Carey Act and the Desert Land Entry transfers.

*Nevertheless, to almost everyone the Sagebrush Rebellion is a
plea for more meaningful participation, for more meaningful partnership between the federal government and the western states in
the establishment of federal land-management policy, which
integrally affects both the West and the remainder of the country.*

Thus, the Sagebrush Rebellion might and might not be many
things. But it is a force, a movement in the West, and in this time of
antifederalist sentiment, it is moving fast. On 2 June 1979 the
Nevada bill was signed by the governor. On 1 July 1979 the Nevada
bill became effective. On 5 September 1979 western attorneys-
general met in Reno to anticipate the legal consequences of this
kind of action in the western states. On 6 and 7 September western
legislators met to share their concepts and enthusiasms. The 17 September cover of *Newsweek* featured the "angry West," and the
article explored ramifications of those management wrinkles and the
Nevada activity. On 29 and 30 October western attorneys-general
met in Seattle to discuss a community of interest, to establish a community of approach in the legal area, to define the Sagebrush
Rebellion. After 1 January 1980 there will be an open season on
Sagebrush Rebellion ideas in the several legislatures of the western
states.

In understanding the issue, it is important to focus on the
Sagebrush Rebellion Nevada style and to acknowledge briefly that
it really occurs in two dimensions: (1) the political/public-relations
dimension (i.e., talking about these frustrations, legislating statutes,
and so on) and (2) the legal dimension (i.e., the test case, the lawsuit
in Nevada). This movement came about, so say the authors of the
bill, to force the federal government to sue the State of Nevada, to
come to the courts in that state, and perhaps to the U.S. Supreme
Court, for a substantive declaration of sovereign rights—sovereign
to the State of Nevada and sovereign to the United States—to determine who will own, manage, and operate the various public-land
interests being disputed in Nevada.

Thus far the focus of the Rebellion has been the extent of
federal ownership. And the extent is somewhat startling. Ninety-
six percent of Alaska is under federal ownership and management;

87 percent of Nevada—a figure that galvanized them into action; 66 percent of Utah; 64 percent of Idaho; and 53 percent of Oregon. In Wyoming, California, and Arizona federal ownership varies between 43 and 48 percent. Colorado, New Mexico, and Montana enjoy (or suffer, depending on your point of view) 30 to 36 percent. And 29 percent of Washington is under federal ownership and management.

Idaho has a total area, including all lands of all types, of 53 million acres. Eighteen different federal agencies manage land in Idaho. The largest holdings are controlled by the Bureau of Land Management (12 million acres) and the Forest Service (20 million acres). By contrast, the state controls 2.7 million acres. (About 19 million acres are in the hands of private parties and local governments.)

Beyond the question of federal ownership, the Rebellion is also an outgrowth of frustration about federal land-management practices. Specifically, that frustration is a product both of restrictive changes—either accomplished or anticipated—in federal land-management policy and of federal failure to deliver on its promises to the states.

It is not as some federal representatives have been inclined to say in recent appearances. It is not a western fraud. It is not the artifice of western politicians. It is the position of the federal government that has changed, not the western people, the western ethic, or the western states.

In 1976 the federal government went almost overnight from a policy of controlled disposition—gradual, careful, occasional sale of federal lands for good and legitimate purposes—to a policy of retaining unappropriated public domain. And that switch in the BLM Organic Act and in the Federal Land Policy and Management Act began precluding, avoiding, abating mineral claims and patents and their development. That switch was frustrating to people who had Carey Act land allocations pending. It was frustrating to those who were moving toward agricultural development under Desert Land entries. They were continually hampered by requirements for environmental-impact statements and RARE II statements, by cutbacks and changes and limitations, by studies, hearings, regulations, and rulings. In the judgment of westerners, this was mismanagement. That whole process and its source—the federal change from a policy of controlled disposition to one of almost absolute retention—

evoked angry reactions at many levels throughout the West. And ultimately that reaction manifested itself in the state legislatures.

As those legislatures began thinking about the redress of some of these grievances, they determined that the proper way to resolve the difficulty would be to force a lawsuit. A lawsuit should clarify the issues of title, management, and sovereignty. In thinking through that, they came up with two constitutional theories that are at the base of the Sagebrush Rebellion: the "equal footing" doctrine, and the "property clauses" or "property restrictions" imposed on the federal government by the Constitution.

The "equal footing" doctrine runs something like this: When the original thirteen colonies and four or five subsequent states entered the Union, they controlled all their unappropriated public domain. (And they still do.) The equal-footing doctrine relates to a term found in most admission bills of the several western states that says something like this: The territory shall be admitted as a state of the Union on a footing equal in all respects with that of the original thirteen colonies. Reasoning perhaps more logically than legalistically, the frustrated western legislators concluded that to the extent that there are large, unappropriated federal public-domain holdings inside the western states, those states are not in all respects equal to the original colonies. And that kind of limitation, they reason, might be overset on a constitutional basis where the federal government chooses to discriminate, or has discriminated, in that way against western states. However, a close look at the doctrine of equal footing reveals a number of loose ends. First, the doctrine has no precise constitutional dimension. In fact, the words appear nowhere in the Constitution of the United States. Rather, the doctrine is a creature of the U.S. Supreme Court under several interpretations. And as a rule, those interpretations have been limited to political rights. Certainly they have not been extended fully to issues of economic standing. Furthermore, the questions regarding a state's ability to waive claims against unappropriated federal domain have been resolved both for and against the state. Logically one can create an argument of some distinction and some discrimination. But to prevail legally, the western states must convince the U.S. Supreme Court that ownership of unappropriated public domain is essential to state sovereignty and that that state sovereignty is, therefore, a right conferred by the United States Constitution not subject to waiver by a state or to any other process.

Accordingly, the equal-footing doctrine figured prominently in the design of this test case. But even Nevada's attorney-general and legislators acknowledge that the doctrine must be extended considerably before it can be prevailed upon as a constitutional basis for the Sagebrush Rebellion.

I mentioned another theory, the "property clause" of the Constitution of the United States. There are actually two property clauses. Article I, Section 8, says, "The Congress shall have Power ... To exercise [authority over federal lands and to acquire the same by purchase] for the erection of Forts, Magazines, Arsenals, dock-Yards and other needful Buildings." Article IV, Section 3, says, "The Congress shall have the power to dispose of... the territory... belonging to the United States." To the western legislators, casting about for some solace in the Constitution, the sum of those two statements is that the limited authority granted Congress to hold land for forts, arsenals, and dockyards is not authority to hold for perpetuity large, unappropriated blocks of public domain without a specific and necessary public purpose in those holdings, consistent with forts, magazines, arsenals, and dockyards. That proposition may be advanced to the court, and it is arguable that the interrelationship of the property clauses and the equal-footing doctrine will be established as a proposition in favor of Nevada. However, as you can see, there are some limitations legally: The application of those constitutional theories to the precise situation which Nevada hopes to raise is as yet fully unestablished in the courts.

There is yet another legal problem complicating the Sagebrush Rebellion. The Idaho Admission Bill, like most state admission bills in the West, contains this disclaimer in its Section 12: "The State of Idaho shall not be entitled to any further or other grants of land for any purpose other than as expressly provided by this act." Article XXI, Section 19, of the Idaho Constitution (adopted at the same time as the Admission Act) makes the same disclaimer more specific: "And the people of the State of Idaho do agree and declare that we forever disclaim all right and title to the unappropriated public lands forever disclaim all right and title to the unappropriated public lands lying within the boundaries thereof." Nevada and Idaho and a number of sister states in the West have similar disclaimers in their admission bills and in their constitutions. Accordingly, the Nevada Constitution Proposition must be that the Constitution of the United States and the limitations on the federal government are so significant and so overwhelming that they allow the federal courts to set aside these specific disclaimers, engineered at the time of territorial statehood in the western states. Thus, there are some legal difficulties.

The first step after having clarified the issues, is to advance the propositions to the courts. And in thinking this through, the western legislatures have come up with several statutory approaches—not a simple, monolithic takeover of all the land, but a number of rather subtle approaches. Let us consider first of all the Nevada approach: By a bill effective 1 July 1979, under the authority of the State Land Registrar and creating a board of review for that purpose, Nevada ruled (1) that all public lands *except* Department of Defense lands, Department of Energy lands, Bureau of Reclamation lands, Indian reservations, Congressionally authorized National Parks and Forests, and certain limited other lands are the property of the State of Nevada and are subject to jurisdiction and control by the state rather than by the federal government, and (2) that environmental care will be addressed by a study commission. The legislature appropriated $125,000 per year for the implementation of the act, and they authorized the preparation of regulations in smoothing that approach. The Nevada Bill, the wholesale-takeover Nevada-style, was designed to produce a test case that would determine whether state or federal sovereignty should prevail in the unappropriated domain (largely Bureau of Land Management land) in Nevada.

California took a second approach: The legislature passed a bill to create a study by the State Lands Commission on whether or not the management and ownership of BLM lands should be vested in state hands. The commission was directed to complete that study 1 July 1980 and to report to the governor, the legislature, and the attorney-general. The attorney-general was thereafter to take appropriate action. That Bill was vetoed by Governor Brown. California has not yet taken another action.

A third approach was taken by Oklahoma. In fact, this approach became effective 9 May 1979—in advance of the effective date of the Nevada legislation. In Oklahoma the legislature required that the federal government (except where it has already obtained consent) seek from the legislature of the State of Oklahoma consent for any federal acquisition had outside municipal boundaries. The U.S. Constitution, in Article I, Section 8, requires that the purchase of land for the erection of those forts and arsenals be preceded by the consent of the state legislature. Amazingly enough, the consent requirement had been forgotten and not often, if ever, sought. The Oklahoma approach, emphasizing that language in the Constitution, tells the federal government, in effect, "We consent to the federal acquisition of land that you had for customs houses and post offices, for stockyards and irrigation purposes, but to the extent that you wish to acquire other state lands for any purpose outside municipal areas, you will, as the federal Constitution requires, seek the permission of the Oklahoma legislature. Without the majority consent, we will not allow you to exercise that acquisition authority inside our state."

A fourth approach, taken by Alaska and Utah, is largely one of memorials and resolutions: memorials to Congress urging federal action in addressing specific statutes; resolutions in support of the Nevada legislature as they go through their legislation, the creation of their commission, and their test case.

A fifth approach, which I shall call the Idaho approach, is rather a hybrid. More than one state legislature will be introducing full Nevada-style bills, and Idaho is no exception. Whether or not that approach is successful, time will tell. But three other things will be done in the Idaho legislature. (In some respects this approach is more sophisticated than that of any other legislature.) First, the legislature will address only specific federal government disputes in Idaho and will engineer a Nevada-style or similar approach to those specific problems. For instance, since 1908 the Idaho and federal governments have been disputing the ownership of phosphate rights in certain lands in southeastern Idaho that were transferred from the federal to the state government by restricted patent. The Idaho legislature could approach this dispute by creating a bill narrower in scope than the broad Nevada-style takeover. This bill would assert the right of Idaho to exercise authority and ownership over those mineral rights, a right the state has claimed but never had litigated or reinstated since 1908. This approach has several strengths. Number one, the state can focus on an issue that is very narrow and depends very little on constitutional precepts and principles. Second, the tight focus enables the courts to litigate swiftly and accurately, which will save money and time. And third, the state can identify issues in which its claim has obvious merit, including specific support in history, law, and fact. Thus, with this specific approach, Idaho can zero in on phosphate rights, the problems associated with the wild and scenic rivers, or the controversy surrounding the state's proposal to expand its legislation regarding birds of prey. And every state's legislature could follow this course rather than the broad, wholesale takeover.

The second prong of Idaho's three-part approach will be to amend the state constitution, striking the language which disclaims any right, title, or interest in unappropriated public domain. The legislature of Idaho may issue a referendum, an opportunity for Idaho residents to vote on whether or not that specific disclaimer ought to be stricken from the Constitution. If the amendment proposal passes the House and Senate, it will be presented to the people of Idaho for their vote. And at the political level, this would have merit, because it would involve the people directly in the question of whether or not the Sagebrush Rebellion, as defined in Idaho, ought to proceed.

Third, the Idaho legislature is contemplating the resolution-and-memorial approach. The resolutions would express not only support for Nevada, they also would recommend that the attorney-general of Idaho participate as *amicus* of the Nevada court once that test case is framed and once it becomes clear that ideas and interests in Nevada are consistent with ideas and interests in Idaho.

Thus, there are several styles of approach, several complexities of approach, in the Sagebrush Rebellion. There simply is not a single, monolithic approach with a single, well-defined objective. The Rebellion is many things, in many forms, to many people.

One difficulty with the Sagebrush Rebellion at this relatively early stage is the number of misconceptions about what it is. In conclusion, I shall list three and discuss them briefly.

The first misconception about the Sagebrush Rebellion is that it is an all-or-none takeover. Even in Nevada that is not so. The concept is useful in generating enthusiastic support from ranchers and others who wish it to be nothing else, and it is useful in making simple arguments about the rape, ruin, and pillage of the land. But the issue is simply *not* all or none. Even Nevada's all-or-none approach was designed specifically so that the federal government would sue the state, so that a test case could be brought to adjust these broad concepts of title and ownership. If successful, that test case probably would result in new definitions, in new limitations on federal management policy, and in a gradual identification and transfer of some marginal lands. Certainly the gradual implementation would be in the interest of the court, as the court defines the problem. And in fact, several of those state approaches that I mentioned seek no immediate transfer. They seek well-defined and careful studies. They seek participation in specific issues rather than wholesale transfers. It is not fair to criticize the Sagebrush Rebellion as being simply an all-or-nothing transfer. It is not that.

Second, some who are opposed to the Sagebrush Rebellion argue that all state lands must be managed so as to produce maximum income. In Idaho that misconception has been urged by its author, the Secretary of the Interior, a senior senator of the State of Idaho, the Idaho Conservation League, and others relatively in the know. But it simply is not so. Idaho does have in its constitution, and most western states have in their constitutions, requirements that school-endowment lands be managed to produce maximum income for the public schools. But the fact is that not all western lands and not all state lands are school-endowment lands. Many lands in Idaho and in other western states are managed for a variety of purposes. There are parks and recreation lands. There is fish and game land. And Idaho has a capitol building in Boise. Those state holdings are managed for many other purposes, some of which have nothing to do with maximizing income. It is not fair to say that the states are mandated by their own constitutions to rape and ruin and

pillage. Lands that the states succeed to or take over do not auto-
matically become school-endowment lands managed for maximum-
income purposes. And even where the states are producing maximum income from school lands, they adopt a relatively enlightened,
multiple-use approach, with deference to the recreational and
environmental values.

The third argument against the Sagebrush Rebellion is that
stage government management would allow ruin or require massive,
thoughtless sell-offs of the land. The state simply would not be able
to handle the job of managing the land. Most of that argument is
based upon the all-or-none theory, which has no validity. But even
if one considers, for instance, that in Idaho the BLM spends $13.1
million to produce $6.2 million in revenue, or that the Forest
Service in Idaho spends $77 million to produce $32 million in
revenue, one simply cannot assume, even on the all-or-none theory,
that the state is incapable of managing with better results and less
investment than the federal government does. But when the
Rebellion is viewed in the proper perspective, the states are well
equipped. That is, if the transfer were gradual, beginning with
marginal lands and other lands held not for reasonable national
purpose, the states would need only to assume some additional
management activities, to assume a more active partnership with
the federal government. (There would be no change of ownership
in some cases.) And the states are well equipped to prevent excesses
and problems that plague the federal government because it lacks
sensitivity to local issues. No economic analysis yet designed would
allow either side to make an intelligent argument. But when that
analysis is available, it will not be based on an all-or-none takeover.
That analysis will not assume that the states must spend as much per
acre on management. The analysis will not assume that they must
take over instantly. But the analysis will assume that the states can
produce more income per acre on some parcels.

In conclusion let me simply say that the Sagebrush Rebellion is
not a single, simplistic movement with each state planning to claim
all federal land on some hypothetical date because of some hypothetical court case. The Rebellion cannot be dismissed following
a parade of horrible speculations about what may or may not happen in that hypothetical instance. The reql question is this: Given
the federal government's sharp break with its own historical policy
of encouraging private enterprise and private development of the

West, is it not time that state and local governments and people assumed a more active role in mitigating or changing national management policies?

This is a revolution of sorts, but a revolution whose first shot is yet to be fired. To the western view, the momentum and the intensity of the movement at this point are a testament of the nobility of the cause.

The Mandate for Multiple Use

Gary Wicks

The attempt to take over federally owned lands in the West, very colorfully termed the "Sagebrush Rebellion," illustrates that while we in the West like to think of ourselves as different, we are just as prone as anyone else to get sidetracked on issues not in our best interest. The Sagebrush Rebellion makes very good press in the East and the West, and it is sure to have support from politicians and other groups. But where is is leading us? Not very far, in my opinion. And certainly not when you consider it in the context of the problems that the West will be facing in the eighties (which I view as a critical period).

Let me say at the outset that I do not see the Sagebrush Rebellion as some do, as simply a land-grab by greedy people whose sole intent is to expropriate public lands. It is the outgrowth of an issue that has long roots in the history of the West—a history of great philosophical and geographical distance from Washington, and of western reluctance to go along with eastern ideas and laws. But the Rebellion was ignited by a number of policies that have come out of Washington in the past few years. The frustrations are directed at the federal government in general and the Bureau of Land Management in particular. And there *are* frustrations. There is a genuine concern about changes in policy and in the management of public lands during the last few years. Before that, public lands were available for all kinds of uses and almost without any management at all. But now management, as required by federal laws, is taking on a larger meaning than simply issuing permits or counting cows. The

Federal Land Policy and Management Act, signed by President Ford in 1976, serves as a focal point for much of this frustration. However, FLiPMA (affectionately so-called by very few) was not a product of some out-of-touch eastern liberal. Western congressmen and ideas played a large role in its content and its passage. Many provisions in the act were based on recommendations made by the Public Land Law Review Commission, which was made up almost completely of western representatives.

FLipMA does represent change. It established that public land should be retained in federal ownership. It obligated the BLM to change from a caretaker agency to a management agency. It mandated a wilderness review of all public lands. It required rules and regulations for activities on public lands. And it meant that decisions about management had to be tied to land-use plans.

At the same time that the provisions of FLiPMA were being implemented, other major programs on the public land were undergoing significant changes. Following a lawsuit with the NRDC, the BLM was obligated to embark on a large-scale effort to complete a number of grazing I and Ss in a short period. These, together with the mandate for multiple use in FLiPMA, reduced stocking rates to grazing capacities of the range. The federal coal program went through a similarly difficult period. After a lawsuit with NRDC, the program came to a halt, and no coal leases could be issued on federal land. We have now modified that, after three or four years of discussions and BISs. That represented a significant change in how the public lands are managed. Now our off-road vehicle uses are coming under control through executive orders from the President and through the requirement for Motor Vehicles Management.

The rapidity of change, the uncertainty over what the changes mean, the frequent inability of BLM to respond to public input, the mistakes made by the federal government in implementing programs—all these are a source of frustration and have reinforced the belief that private ownership is preferable. But many people are involved in the Sagebrush Rebellion for less defensible reasons. Some see an opportunity to capitalize on the availability of private lands in the West, and certainly it affords an opportunity for political advantage.

The Sagebrush Rebellion has been proceeding on two fronts. One is legal. This is exemplified by the approach in Nevada, where the state legislature passed a law saying simply that federal lands are now state lands. The direct appropriation approach. Similar bills have been introduced in other states. And we expect that they will be introduced, and perhaps passed, in yet others. The second approach, at the federal level, is represented by Senator Hatch's Bill 1680, which would convey to the states all federally owned lands, including Forest Service lands. Unlike the Nevada approach, though, Senator Hatch's Bill is based on the recognition that the lands are federally owned and that it would take an act of Congress to effect a change. I do not agree that either approach will be successful. The first, the appropriation of federal land, is based on a pretty hollow legal argument. The second approach is in for a difficult debate that even the bill's principal sponsor admits will stretch out over at least ten years. (And I doubt that it has much opportunity for success.) Not only are there philosophical problems with the bill, but it is pretty hard to believe—when we are going through an energy crisis and when we recognize that the public lands contain the bulk of the nation's coal, oil and gas, geothermal energy and oil shale—that the federal government will turn those lands over to an uncertain future and uncertain management.

Why then should we even treat the Sagebrush Rebellion seriously, and why should the current approach be thought detrimental to agriculture in the West? There are I believe a couple of good answers to these questions. The first is that the problems to be faced by the West and by agriculture over the next ten to twenty years are critical to the survival of both in the form that we know them. We in the West need all available political and other resources if we are to solve these problems in our favor. We need to strengthen the unity now emerging on some of these issues. We need to learn how to use our water, how to develop our energy, how to deal with the social and economic impacts both good and bad that are going to follow that development. Idaho's attorney-general has said that the Rebellion is not an "all-or-nothing" issue. But like it or not, most people will see it as "all or nothing." And that is going to divide the West as much as it will divide the East from the West. That division of political and other resources, that reduction of ability to solve our problems, is something the West can ill afford.

Second, in dealing with public lands (after years of uncertainty created in large measure by the implementation of many programs), we will be facing at least ten years of uncertainty, with litigation and injunctions but without decisions about how to develop our resources or what resources to develop, and without funding for needed improvements. This uncertainty will affect everyone—from environmentalists to oil companies. Nobody will know who must or how to get approval for activities on public land. This uncertainty will bring just about all public-land activities to a standstill. In fact, if I were a no-growth advocate, I would see the Sagebrush Rebellion as an almost perfect way to achieve my wishes for a long time.

Congressional response to past efforts like the Sagebrush Rebellion has been to enact laws that are more detailed and less flexible, with added requirements for Congressional involvement in state and local affairs. So the effort to bring attention to the problems that some users of public lands are facing in the West may become a long, bitter struggle over ownership of those lands. Instead of resolving the real issues, it will leave us worse off than before. And agriculture in particular will suffer.

There are many arguments for and against turning federal lands over to private ownership. But these arguments concern themselves with the impact of such a turnover—the *end result*. What I am arguing is that the *process*, as represented by the Sagebrush Rebellion, will have a long lasting detrimental effect on the West.

If there were no alternative, I might support such a process. But there is a better way to solve the problems and ease the frustrations. We can reduce the uncertainty regarding use of public lands, address the inequalities, improve federal responsiveness to state and local concerns. In fact, that process has already begun. For instance, the coal program is being worked out in cooperation with the governors of all the western states. This program recognizes the legitimate concerns of various interest groups and allows for the continuing participation of state and local governments. The result will be an appropriate leasing of coal. Similarly, Congress has passed laws and implemented a policy of recognizing the importance of state and local government recommendations regarding public lands. This is a policy that I argued for in Washington and that in some small measure I helped bring to fruition. It is a policy I intend to implement in Utah, and it is a policy that the BLM followed before the birth of the Sagebrush Rebellion.

Together we can solve our problems. Wilderness is one of our principal concerns. By 1980 all the lands that are being inventoried will be identified as "nonwilderness" or as "wilderness-study areas."

And once we get into the wilderness-study phase, the BLM will, in accord with the law, consider the concerns of state and local people. We will consider the potential impact of wilderness designation on the local economy and will make our recommendations accordingly.

The attorney-general mentioned the inability to transfer lands from public ownership to state and private hands. In reality there is no inability. The Federal Land Policy and Management Act provides for exchanges and in-lieu selections. It provides for sales. In fact, in Nevada the BLM has had a number of sales that transferred public land to private ownership. If there are areas where a transfer is necessary, the law provides for that. What we need to do is being done on the legal side of the Sagebrush Rebellion: We must identify specific problems and go to work on them, involving the state and local governments. And I have a great deal of confidence that if we carry that message back to Congress, we will obtain a legislative or policy resolution. We have done it before. We can do it again— as long as we have a common purpose.

I would like to end on a personal note. I grew up in the West. I spent some time in the southern states and on the East Coast, but I believe that living in the West is best. And I am convinced that a large part of the reason for the superiority of the West is the availability of public lands. And in spite of the legal theory of equal footing, I would not change places with one person on the East Coast or anywhere else where there is no public ownership of land. Nobody who spends any time in the state of New York can argue that we are worse off than they are. But if we are in fact less than equal, I will still take what we have in preference to what they have. There is a sense of freedom about being able to go elk hunting for about fifteen dollars a year, of being able to fish in miles of open stream, of being able to stake mining claims and graze cattle on public land. A sense of freedom comes from the solitude we can find on public lands. These are freedoms I do not want to lose. And whether I am in or out of government, I intend to do what I can to preserve that heritage for my children.

Fencing Out the Majority

Cecil D. Andrus

An attempt is being made to hornswoggle all Americans out of a unique land heritage which has been a bulwark of our society and the source of a special freedom that has made the West such a great place to live. The threat is from the so-called Sagebrush Rebellion, which has the potential of transforming the West from a land of open spaces into a patchwork eyesore that benefits the few and fences out the majority.

Promoters of the Sagebrush Rebellion claim they are striking a blow for states' rights and equality. They say the West is being discriminated against because there are large tracts of federal land in the West but not in the East. They argue that the federal government should hand over more than 600 million acres to the states. That would be a disastrous mistake for virtually all Americans whether they are in Nevada, Colorado, Idaho, New York, or Rhode Island.

The land, which some state officials would confiscate, belongs to all the people of this country—not just to some of them, nor even just to the people in the state where the land is located. This means that every American owns more than two-and-a-half acres of public lands of this country, although the deed is not in individual names. No American, regardless of how poor he or she may be, is landless. This has had, and continues to have, a great stabilizing effect on our society.

Unlike the huge private estates and hunting preserves of the rich and powerful, as in Europe and other regions of the world, our federal lands are truly public. They are a legacy of freedom and openness for our children and grandchildren. They have contributed much to our people's feelings about what makes this country unique. Those of us who live in the West have been especially fortunate. Because most of this public land is in our states, we have enjoyed the use, not only of our own two-and-a-half acres, but of land that is part of the heritage of millions of other Americans.

At times we may be irritated by the way federal agencies have managed the land. We may disagree with restrictions put on the use of some of the land. We may see instances in which the resources could be better used for economic development. But by and large we have ample room and freedom for hunting and fishing, for camping, for grazing cattle, for prospecting for fun and profit, and for hundreds of other activities denied to people who live in the non-public-land states. Federal-land watersheds give westerners good water and electric power, and their clean air contributes greatly to the special western quality of life.

Leaders of the Sagebrush Rebellion are upset that the nineteenth-century policy advocating disposal of federal public lands was formally repealed in 1976 and replaced by a policy intended to maintain the public lands for the greatest public good. Actually, a series of laws dating back to the turn of the century had made the giveaway theory obsolete. The Federal Land Policy and Management Act of 1976 simply acknowledged this fact.

It should be evident that what some ardent backers of the Sagebrush Rebellion seek is an easy avenue for transferring land from public to private ownership. And because few states would find it feasible to manage these big areas soundly, they could be forced to sell it off, piece by piece, giving special economic interests their opportunity to profit. There is no good guarantee that the public will share or be compensated, and there is great danger that the land and the people will suffer as a result of special-interest efforts to reap short-term profits without concern for the future.

State officials, regardless of good intentions, would find it hard to resist the overwhelming pressures to sell off the public lands. Some state officials would have little choice. For example, in Idaho the State Constitution says state lands must be managed for the highest return to the school-endowment fund. If they followed that to the letter, as the State Land Board must do, it would mean a lot of those lands would be sold, or leased, for harvest—either timber or

mineral. Eventually the land would be carved up, fenced, and
posted where it is now generally open for public use, both recreational and economic.

State efforts to take over management of public lands—if they
genuinely tried to manage these lands—would deplete state trea-
suries. It is doubtful that, in this time when taxpayers are more
than a little restless, the state governments would be willing or able
to levy taxes sufficient to cover the cost of management now borne
by the federal government. Even the leading state officials in land
management have conceded privately that the burden would be
overwhelming.

Fortunately, there is no sound legal basis for the state challenge to federal ownership and management of the public lands. As
the western states entered the Union, they were given portions of
federal lands upon which to build economic bases. In return, each of
the states recognized the right of the federal government to retain
ownership of the remaining unappropriated public lands. There was
a sound reason for this. The public-domain lands of the West were
acquired by the national government through purchase and warfare, at the expense of all Americans living at that time. Since then
they have always been federally owned. These conditions were well
understood and accepted by all westerners then.

Now some state officials want to renege.

It is hard to believe they are serious, or that this is much more than political rhetoric. But the federal government is a popular target for criticism everywhere, and especially in the West. So the Sagebrush Rebellion has picked up at least lip service even in states outside of its native Nevada. Thoughtful westerners will avoid jumping on this bandwagon. Those who have joined should give some further thought to the detrimental consequences of the proposal.

Federal management of public lands is far from perfect. Each of us who deals or has dealt with federal programs and bureaucracy can recommend changes to make it better. That is what we should be working to do—to provide federal management that is more responsive to local needs and wishes, where that is compatible with the national interest and the future of the resources and the people involved.

Winston Churchill once commented that democracy was not a very good form of government—but that all others were worse. That may well be true of federal management of the public lands; for all its faults, the current system is superior to all alternatives proposed to date.

Certainly the Sagebrush Rebellion is a step backward, not forward, in our efforts to manage America's resources wisely. Most important, it would begin a massive erosion of the freedom traditionally associated with the West.

Notes and References

NOTES TO INTRODUCTION

1. Wendell Berry, *The Unsettlling of America: Culture and Agriculture* (San Francisco), 1977, p. 43.

2. Letter from Alvin Josephy to Richard Hart.

3. Thadis W. Box, "The Arid Lands Revisited: 100 Years after John Wesley Powell," *57th Annual Faculty Lecture*, Utah State University (Logan, Utah), 1978.

4. Wire service report.

5. *Minidoka County News* (Rupert, Idaho), November 1 1979.

6. Steve Forrester, "Sagebrush Rebellion May Go Nowhere in Congress," *Times News* (Twin Falls, Idaho), December 15 1979, p. A9.

7. *Ibid.*

8. *Ibid.*

9. Doug Underwood, "U.S. Urges Nevada Suit Over Land," *Idaho Statesman* (Boise, Idaho), February 6 1980, p. 10B.

10. Press release.

11. *Times News*, February 9 1980.

NOTES TO CHAPTER 2:   THE ENERGY CRISIS
AND THE NORTHERN GREAT PLAINS

1. Ministry of the Environment, *Parliamentary Report* 44 (Oslo, Norway), 1975–76, p. 2; see also Ministry of the Environment, *Acid Precipitation and Its Effects in Norway* (Oslo), 1974.

2. Svante Oden, "The Acidification of Air and Precipitation and Its Consequences on the Natural Environment," *Ecology Committee Bulletin* 1, 1968; see also *Scientific American*, October 1979, pp. 43–51.

3. "Hydrological Effects of Strip Mining Near Decker, Montana" (Montana Bureau of Mines), 1974; and "Rehabilitation of Western Coal Lands" (National Academy of Sciences, Washington, D.C.), 1973.

4. For a solid review of in situ uranium mining, see Donald Snow, "In Situ Uranium Mining: The Process and the Problems," *Down to Earth*, September/October 1973.

5. "The powers not delegated to the United States by the constitution nor prohibited to it by the states are reserved to the states respectively or to the people."

NOTES TO CHAPTER 4: THE QUANTITY AND QUALITY OF
FARMLAND IN THE ROCKY MOUNTAIN REGION

1. A. A. Klingebiel and P. H. Montgomery, "Land-Capability Classification," *USDA Handbook* (Washington, D.C.), 1961, p. 210.

2. United States Department of Agriculture, Soil Conservation Service, "Land Inventory and Monitoring," Memorandum, 15 October 1975.

3. United States Census Bureau, *1974 Census of Agriculture*, vol. 2, part 9 (Washington, D.C.), 1975.

4. United States Department of the Interior, "Critical Water Quality Problems Facing the Eleven Western States," Report of the Westwide Water Study (Washington, D.C.), 1975.

5. United States Department of Agriculture, Economics, Statistics, and Cooperative Service, *Who Owns the Land?* (Washington, D.C.), 1979.

6. United States General Accounting Office, *Changing Character and Structure of American Agriculture: An Overview*, CED–78–178 (Washington, D.C.), 1978.

7. Neil Sampson, *Agricultural Land Conversion: Results of a National Survey*, Statistical Bulletin 317 (Washington, D.C.: National Association of Conservation Districts), in press.

8. James M. Jeffords, "Protecting Farmland: Minimizing the Federal Role," *Journal of Soil and Water Conservation*, 34(4): 158–59.

NOTES TO CHAPTER 5:   CAN THE FAMILY FARM SURVIVE?

1. Idaho Statewide FARM Survey, 1979.

2. Vera J. Banks, "Farm Population Trends and Farm Statistics," United States Department of Agriculture, *Rural Development Research Report* 3 (Washington, D.C.), 1978.

3. Ellis Armstrong, "This is One World," talk delivered before the Salt Lake City Rotary Club, March 7 1978.

4. Report by the Wasatch Front Regional Council to the Salt Lake County Commission, *The Deseret News* (Salt Lake City), April 30 1979.

NOTE TO CHAPTER 7:   THE 160-ACRE LIMITATION

1. The legislation, chiefly sponsored by Senator Frank Church, to completely revamp the 1902 Reclamation Act, was still pending as of May 1980.

NOTES TO CHAPTER 13: ECONOMIC REALITIES

1. Idaho State FARM Survey, 1979.

2. Frank LeRoux, *The Myth of Agricultured Prosperity* (Walla Walla, Washington), 1976.

3. Wendell Berry, *The Unsettling of America: Culture and Agriculture* (San Francisco), 1977.

4. Idaho State FARM Survey, 1979.